A Different Shade of Seeing

Elizabeth Brennan

A catalogue record for this book is available from the National Library of Australia

Copyright © 2019 Elizabeth Brennan

All rights reserved.

ISBN-13: 978-1-922343-01-7

Linellen Press
265 Boomerang Road
Oldbury, Western Australia
www.linellenpress.com.au

Acknowledgments

There are many people who played a huge role in the creation of the book. Some would be aware of their support, others not; some have passed away; some I have lost track of.

In a brief timeline of those who would be unaware, I include the nuns who taught me in primary school, who first laid the seed, who planted a question as to who I might be; my maternal grandfather, the first person to introduce me to the poetry of Christopher Brennan, my great-uncle, from which developed a longing to know about my Irish heritage; Fr. Tom Gaine, a dear friend with whom I worked for over twenty years and who accompanied me on my journey throughout Ireland.

Again, there were many who gave great encouragement and assistance in the actual writing of the book. Members of the Karrinyup Writer's Club, in particular Dorothy Duperouzel who, without knowledge, inspired the beginning of the book and the title; dear friends Jenny McNae and Maureen Helen and members of the FAWWA Long Book Club; Fred Rae and Colin Merrey from The Irish Scene who both encouraged and supported and corrected some mistakes!

To Shane McCauley who assisted me in innumerable ways in encouragement and challenge, assessment, proofreading and editing.

And last – but certainly not least – my foremost encouragers and inspirers? My family.

Thank you to all – if I have missed anyone, rest assured you are deep in my heart.

For permission to reproduce copyright material, the publishers are grateful to the following:

Extracts from Axel Clarke's *Christopher Brennan: A Critical Biography* (1980), printed with permission of Melbourne University Press, Carlton, Victoria.

Poem *I am Kerry* - Copyright: The Estate of Sigerson Clifford, 1986. Reprinted with kind permission of Mercier Press, Ireland.

Poem, *the Famine Year*, by Jane Francesca Elgee '*Speranza*', 1821-1896

Laugh Kookaburra Laugh, Rainbow Coloured Birds, and *The Sisters* from *The Dreaming of Aboriginal Australia* by Jean A. Ellis (2006) printed with permission of Kaliarna Productions Pty. Ltd. Penrith NSW.

Extracts from Hyland, John (1993), *Do you know us at all?*: P.A.C.T.T. *Promoting attitudinal change towards travellers*, Parish of the Travelling people, Dublin. Printed with permission.

Poem, *To a Mountain*, by Henry Kendall (1993*), Songs from the Mountains*, William Maddock; London: Sampston Low, Marston, Searle and Rivington, Sydney.

Extracts from Sean Maher (1998) *The Road to God Knows Where: a memoir of a travelling boyhood*, printed with permission of Veritas Publications, Dublin.

Extract from a speech by Sister Delores O'Sullivan printed with kind permission of the Holy Spirit Missionary Sisters, Aspley, Queensland.

Quote from *The Shadow King* printed with the kind permission of Tom E. Lewis.

Black Stones Around the Green Shamrock – a poetry anthology by and about Travellers, compiled by Michael O'Reilly and Máirín Kenny, Blackrock Teachers' Centre.

Extracts from *Travelling Man* and *The Reading Lesson* from *High Island* by Richard Murphy, printed with the permission of Richard Murphy and Faber and Faber Ltd.

Contents

Acknowledgments iii

Contents v

Preface vii

Prologue ix

One 1

Two 5

Three 17

Four 23

Five 42

Six 51

Seven 69

Eight 86

Nine 96

Ten 110

Eleven 128

Twelve 139

Thirteen 159

Fourteen 185

Fifteen 201

Sixteen 213

Ending 224

About the Author 228

Preface

I couldn't have been happier with responses to *A Different Shade of Seeing* when it was released through Equilibrium Books in 2014. My journey towards recognition and understanding of my Irish heritage was deeply personal, so it was humbling that other readers found parts of that story to engage with in their own ways.

I was therefore delighted, five years later, to meet Helen Iles from Linellen Press and to begin discussions with her about re-releasing the book. Through this conversation, I shared my disappointment that more photographs hadn't made it into the first edition. To my delight, Helen responded that she saw no reason this couldn't be rectified. Hence readers will find a few differences between this and the original. In order to include the photos, I have deleted some paragraphs of text. I do not believe these edits in any way detract from the story I share so eagerly with you, and in fact believe the additional images will be attractive to new readers.

Thank you, Helen, for working with me on this.

Elizabeth Brennan, 2019

Prologue

And Yahweh said to Moses: Here I am. Take off your shoes, for the place on which you stand is holy ground.

Totally unbidden, tears flow. I reach for a handkerchief from my handbag on the seat next to me and dab my eyes. A mysterious force tugs me, compels me to stop. I drive on a little further, look for a level piece of ground on the side of the winding mountain road.

I park the car, tentatively step out and arch my head upwards at the rocky mountain slopes behind me. Their grandiose face is now a reassuring familiarity. I bow my head, revere their majesty. I turn and look down at the mist-blanketed valley below. The silence hugs me. I weep. Desperate to identify the source of my tears, I raise my face to the waning sun and mouth a supplication.

Truly, who am I? From whence do I come?

The valley whispers in reply, the mountains comfort me with song. Together, they give voice to my tears.

One

When I boarded the plane at Heathrow in mid-May 2004 for the last leg of my long journey from Australia to Ireland, I was disappointed to find the window seat I had requested situated directly over the wing. As we flew over the Irish Sea, I craned my neck to catch my first glimpse of the coast. My vision blocked, I sat back and closed my eyes. Immediately, I was filled with a deep but gentle *presence* that seemed to permeate my whole being. I was not afraid and had no desire to question what – or who – was this strange phenomenon. I remained leaning back, eyes closed. I was not afraid. I was at complete peace.

Was it only twenty-four or so hours ago since I waved farewell to four of my adult children at Perth Airport? I flushed with embarrassment at the memory of their collective burst in song as I manoeuvred my way into the final departure lounge: *When Irish eyes are smiling* …

I slept fitfully on route to Singapore; relaxed, quite unexpectedly, during the long flight to London.

I opened my eyes and attempted once again to catch sight of the Irish coast. Defeated, I leaned back into my seat. Though the excitement I experienced in various guises throughout the long flight continued to simmer, I succumbed to the quiet, peaceful *presence* that silently, firmly had taken hold.

Little was mentioned, during my childhood, of my Irish heritage. That is not to say I was totally unaware of things Irish in my formative years. The Sisters of St. Joseph ran the local Catholic school where I spent my first seven years schooling and although the Congregation is an Australian Order, most of the nuns were Irish. Their Irishness smothered the students. Both St. Patrick's and St. Joseph's Feast Days – the 17 and 19 March respectively – were holidays, a happy occurrence I gloated about with the neighbourhood children who attended the local State School. The old parish priest was Irish as was the assistant priest. In line with the Australian Catholic Church which, at least up until the 1960s, was certainly an Irish one – the majority of its bishops and clergy Irish – we were taught an Irish theology which was strictly adhered to in the home. Of course, I could not enunciate that at such an early age.

I loved the annual parish end-of-year concert in the school hall: an abundance of Irish singing and dancing. My feet tapped noisily under the seat, much to my mother's chagrin. I shot jealous eyes stage-ward at the dancing girls, frustrated that Mother would not allow me to join the Irish dancing class, an annoyance magnified some years later when my younger sister, Theresa, was so permitted. My jealousy extended to Patricia O'Brien, the most popular girl in school; such envy abated somewhat when she included me in her close circle of friends, a guest at her annual birthday party – on 17 March, to be sure. I devoured Irish mythology and fairy stories from the local library.

Both my paternal great-grandparents were Irish Catholics. They were both in their early 20s when they migrated to Sydney; most likely they did not know each other until they were both in New South Wales. For reasons I was unable to understand or appreciate till many years later, my father offered no clue that might satisfy my youthful, though as yet unrecognised, hunger for identity.

In my last years of high school at Monte Sant' Angelo in North Sydney – again run by an Irish Order, the Sisters of Mercy – one of the elderly nuns introduced me to Irish history and stirred my need to find my own place in the world, to tap into my roots; ignited a dream to walk in the steps of my forebears. The problem: I still did not know fully what or where those roots lay.

When I left school, I completed a one-year course in Secretarial Duties at North Sydney Technical School. After a two-year stint as a stenographer with a law firm, I enrolled in St. Vincent's Hospital to study nursing. The young chaplain to the hospital from the parish of Darlinghurst befriended me. Of course, he was Irish, recently having arrived in Australia after his ordination. We remained friends during my years at St. Vincent's and he introduced me to Irish literature, in particular, the work of Padraig Pearce, one of the leaders of the 1916 Dublin Uprising, which was the catalyst for the subsequent War of Independence, Civil War and eventual declaration of a republic in 1949.

Often when I finished a shift, I rang the door-chime of the presbytery that was next door to the hospital.

'Michael,' the priest who answered the door would call. 'Your girlfriend's here to see you!'

It was to Fr. Michael to whom I confided the confusion and embarrassment I experienced during one of the monthly dances held in the basement of the nurses' quarters to which the young medical students were invited. Ensconced in a progressive barn dance, a tall young man asked my name.

'Brennan,' he exclaimed. 'What a lovely French name!'

My face turned crimson, my voice stuck in my throat. *Am ... am I French!!* My mother's voice, her love of all things exotic, immobilised me. I faltered, slunk from the dance floor.

On my telling, Michael smiled, held my hand and proclaimed definitely: 'No, my dear. You are Irish!'

The seemingly elusive dream to connect with my tenuous roots, sustained me – often quietly, at other times with a screaming urgency – through sixty-one years adrift in a desert of relative *unknowing*.

The captain's voice broke through the recorded music; informed us that the descent to Cork Airport had begun. I stretched forward, glimpsed scenes from an ingrained imagination: fields of various colours of green and yellow, neatly clipped hedges and low walls of grey rock.

Will Tom be changed? I wondered, speculating on the three years since I had seen him.

For nearly twenty years, I had worked with Tom Gaine in the unofficial capacity as pastoral assistant in the Catholic parish of Girrawheen, of which he was the inaugural parish priest in 1979. Not that I ever received 'official' recognition of my role, which evolved slowly. There were no paradigms in the Catholic Church at the time to define the work of a lay person, particularly a lay woman and a divorced one, at that.

On the death of his brother in 2000, Tom returned to Ireland for eight months to take on the responsibility of finalising the family estate. This was a tedious task as his brother was unmarried: hence, there were no heirs. On Tom's retirement and relocation to Ireland in 2001, my work in the parish also ceased.

I stepped from the airport, one hand pulling my luggage, the other clasped comfortably by the benign *presence* I first encountered on the plane.

'Hi, Liz,' Tom said with a bear hug. 'Welcome to Ireland. Let's go to Lyssyclerig.'

Tom had suffered from shingles in the previous twelve months. I knew he had undergone a lot of pain; I expected to see him looking frailer since the last time I had seen him. He looked okay. A bit greyer, a little more stooped, but the gleam in his eye was still evident. And my old friend was pleased to see me!

As we strode to his car, I silently affirmed: *I am on Irish soil. Finally.*

Little did I know the *presence* was to be my faithful companion, would steadfastly walk with me over the next three months of pilgrimage.

Two

On arriving at Lissyclerig, after a two-hour drive from Cork City, Tom suggested I might like a rest. No way! We went for a *walk up the road*, an Irish phrase I soon readily incarnated.

With the region's plentiful supply of rain, the roadside is lush. As well as many varieties of ivy, gigantic fuchsia bushes and heather grow wild. Amazed at the depth of the different shades of the pink and red fuchsia flowers, I bemoaned my inability to grow fuchsia back home. I am always so jealous of Perth friends' beautiful hanging baskets of deep red fuchsia. I have never discovered the reason why my attempts to replicate the same glorious displays are so dismal. As I bent over and breathed in the fragrance, I wondered if I might give it another try.

Rhododendrons, imported into Ireland from England in the mid eighteenth century, crowded the hillsides, their blooms stretched towards the sun. As an invasive species, *Rhododendron ponticum* represents one of the greatest threats facing native woodlands in Ireland. Its presence, I was told by some locals, can have a dramatic effect on the woodland ecosystem, suppressing native ground flora and the natural regeneration of trees and shrubs. Massive efforts are taken year round to slash the rapid growth. I must admit, I did love the beautiful soft mauve rhododendron flowers together with the masses of fuschia bushes thronged along the roadways, particularly in the south of Ireland

Over the many years we worked side by side, in times of rest and relaxation, Tom fascinated me with anecdotes of his youth, of the divergent neighbours and families of Lissyclerig. And here I was, taking *a walk up the road* as Tom pointed out landmarks and farms, the names of which were so familiar. Sadly, many of the families have long since departed from Lissyclerig, either because of death or migration.

Tom's mother's maiden name was O'Sullivan, a common name in southern Kerry. In order to avoid any mix-up with the different families, it was usual practice to attach a nickname to each. Two such families were the O'Sullivan Torys and the Sullivan Pads. Danny Tory lived about half a kilometre from the Gaine farm. Many of the men in the glen were unmarried; they cut their own turf, mowed the hay, sowed potatoes and vegetables and kept their cabins clean.

I used to laugh and take delight as Tom spun tales about *scoreacting* – the Irish word for visiting. It was the sole social life in the glen, in particular for the men who lived on their own. Of an evening, they visited neighbours' homes, sat by the fire, wove yarns, played cards, indulged in a dance or two. The stakes for cards were very high indeed – a few shillings, maybe a goose or two!

Danny's sense of humour, his love of song and his talent with the accordion were renowned, so his neighbours eagerly and expectantly opened their doors to his usual greeting: *God bless all here*. As he settled himself beside the turf fire in the kitchen, the main room in all the cabins, he proceeded to fill his pipe before regaling the household with the latest local gossip, the plight of the animals, which cows had calved, his visits to Kenmare and the people he had met. With a great liking for a wee drop, Danny would go home, fortified and strengthened with the knowledge he was loved by all. In like manner, the local children, who loved to hear him sing, were confident of a warm reception whenever they visited him.

In those years, from the early 1920s to the 1960s, when migration was rampant, it was not easy for the men left alone to tend the farm.

Loneliness and the solitary hard work left its toll. On the few occasions when a local lady visited Danny in his home – an occurrence inevitably noticed by his neighbours – it gave occasion for much innocent – or not so innocent? – banter.

A social event always looked forward to by the families of the glen was the Stations. Twice a year, in the autumn and again in spring, the priest from Kenmare would come to the designated cabin to hear Confessions and say Mass. Preparations went on for days and the house would be cleaned and scrubbed and a feast prepared. Early in the day, friends and neighbours gathered. A sober piety descended on the congregation while the priest heard Confessions and celebrated Mass. Immediately afterwards, however, the food and drink came out and the serious matters of the day ensued: drinking and eating and singing and dancing and more drinking interspersed with the telling of stories. Ah, indeed, a great day was had by all!

As we continued our *walk up the road,* Tom related an incident during a holiday from the seminary in Kilkenny in the mid-1950s. Tom met Danny in Kenmare at the Old Post Office corner, a favourite spot for the men to congregate and chat and watch the world go by. As the church bell rang for the midday Angelus, a time when the people usually stopped and made the Sign of the Cross and the men tipped their hats, Danny, with a devilish glint in his eye, threw his hat to the ground and, in loud voice, shouted: *May God blast us all!*

Another of Danny's neighbours, 'Long Jim' Palmer, was the legendary leader of the Lissy Boys, a wild, tough lot. Well-known for his ability to throw the stone, a favourite sport with the men, he could not resist the temptation to show off his skill with the lads gathered by the Old Post Office corner. When he spied one of the locals walking home with a pot on his head – no doubt for boiling his potatoes – Long Jim picked up a stone, aimed, hit his target spot on. The pot shattered and the poor man slunk down the street, too cowed to retaliate.

We passed the derelict cabin where Katie 'Crutchy' Leary and her mother, Abby, lived. Born with a defective leg, which she tucked under her skirt, Katie became very deft with her crutch. Never married, she was famous for her generosity to the local men who visited her. She was equally famed for her ability to whack a neighbour's goose on the head and sneak it home whenever a good meal took her fancy.

On one occasion, Tom had born the brunt of Crutchy's wrath. On his way home from school with his brother, the boys noticed their cows trespassing in a neighbour's property. As they attempted to steer the cows to their side of the road, Katie, shouting obscenities, approached them and lunged out with her crutch and hit Tom on the head. For no other reason than to dissuade a repetition of the incident, Tom's parents laid a formal complaint.

The day in court caused much excitement in the town, as no one had ever taken umbrage with Katie before. Although everyone was wary of her, including the judge, she was found guilty and fined the grand sum of one shilling and put on a two year good behaviour bond. After the hearing, she strode – if it can be so called – towards Tom and his father at the Old Post Office corner, brandished her crutch and yelled to Tom's father: *Many's the time I left your prick hangin' on the fence, Tom Gaine!*

Another episode that caused much jest among the locals was when Katie, caught in the act of stealing some grocery items from the local school teacher, retorted: *Oh, don't worry. And didn't you leave your overcoat hangin' by the door this mornin' as you was leavin'?*

Tom often drove Katie and her mother, Abby, to town in the horse and cart. Invariably, Crutchy generously enhanced Tom's sex education with tales of her exploits. On one occasion, another young unmarried neighbour, Hannah, joined the two women. As Tom drove, he was privy to the conversation. Or rather, the dual monologues. Katie and Abby spent the whole time educating

Hannah on the private parts of her anatomy and what she should do with them!

Paddy Sullivan Jug lived in Lower Lissyclerig in a worker's cottage. Although he had never been to school and was neither able to read or write, he nevertheless was known as the greatest story teller in the district. Esteemed for his great ability to mow hay and corn with the scythe, he earned a few shillings and a hearty meal from working at the locals' farms. Unfortunately, not everyone paid his due. As he sat in the Gaine kitchen one evening, Paddy vented his anger about a distant neighbour. After he had worked hard on the farm all day, the lady of the house deemed it unnecessary to give him even a cup of tea. *Ah, Missus,* he exclaimed between bites on his thick jam toast and gulps of hot tea. *There she was – out in the cow house – with a four-pronged pike in her hands and shoes up to her arse, pikin' shit out the window. I tell ye, Missus, did I ever have trouble keepin' me mouth shut! I knew what shit needed pikin'!*

Neighbours and friends lived community to the fullest. It was impossible for one farmer to save the hay or cut all his turf by himself. When the weather smiled, the men gathered in *meathals,* busy bees of six to eight men, and accomplished the work in a single day, only to meet at another farm on the morrow. At the end of the day, the billy was boiled, the drink flowed freely, fortified with plenty of homemade cakes and bread and butter and jam.

Tom and I stopped and wandered through the old stone walls that were the only remnants of the two-storey cottage in which Jerry Doyle lived alone, a cottage that was always open to the many Travellers, Ireland's gypsies. Unable to say *No* to anyone, Jerry allowed them to come and go as they liked. They sometimes slept on the settee or bench, although more often on the floor in front of the open kitchen hearth. Jerry owned a jennet, a cross between a donkey and a horse. He often happily loaned his animal to the neighbours. A welcomed visitor to the Gaine home, during his consumption of a hot bowl of soup, he'd mutter repeatedly, *Very soothin', Missus. Very healin'. Very nourishin'.* A shy man, Jerry was not one for going to Church. Like many of the men who lived and worked alone, he did not think he was dressed appropriately. Men such as Jerry and Danny lived out their Catholic faith in their own way.

When Tom first met Jerry on the road after his Ordination, following tradition, Jerry immediately dropped to his knees to receive a blessing. Touched deeply by this simple gesture, and aware of the big part the ageing man had played in his formative years and his undoubted knowledge of the youthful Tom's pranks and escapades, his faults and failings, doubts and fears, Tom knew that Jerry's mark of respect was as much a tribute to his parents and the kindness they showed Jerry as it was for the newly-ordained priest.

We stopped by the shell of the old, one-room, Goulane School, Tom's first. Not able to open the rusted gate, we scrambled over the fence, densely covered with creepers. Although the roof had fallen many years previously, the thick stone walls stood as sentinels over the laughter and songs of the children of long ago. Silently, we stood in the middle of the room, our feet firm on the damp earthen floor, ivy and wild ferns abundant. Before we climbed the fence again, Tom showed me the steep slope behind the school where he had enjoyed skating down in his bare feet. At the base of the slope, the assistant priest, on one of his regular visits to the school, taught the lads the manly art of boxing! A pugilist at heart, Tom laughed as he recalled how he readily dropped his bags to strike the first blow at any opportunity.

Still further along, Tom showed me the empty patch where his aunty Lizzy Gaine lived with her husband, Jack Kissane, and family. Invariably, when Tom visited the house, Lizzy asked him to make her a *nice pot of tea, darlin'*. When he gave his aunt her tea, she invariably remonstrated: *Oh me darlin'! It's gotta be hot! It's gotta be really boilin'. Put it back on the fire. Let it really boil, me darlin'.*

Tom and his cousin, Joe Kissane, often went to the wasteland to bring home a deer. Leaving home about 4 am, they were sometimes joined by Murt O'Shea, whose family lived in the last farm in the glen which was next to Lord Kenmare's estate, a certain spot for finding a deer. The lads had to be sure of their shot as the echo of the blast would certainly alert the gamekeeper who would head off as soon as he heard it to catch the culprits. On one occasion, having secured their catch, the boys hid it under some heather. They spent the remainder of the day exploring the mountains. When they returned to claim their prize, they spied the gamekeeper on a cliff above. Tails between their legs, they were forced to leave their prize behind.

A neighbour, Mikey 'Batt' Sullivan, had married a girl from the Black Valley, a remote, breathtakingly beautiful valley at the foot of the McGillicuddy Reeks, on the other side of Moll's Gap on the Kenmare/Killarney Road. The only source of merriment and social life for the families who farmed their sheep on the mountainside was each other. It was not unusual for families in the valley to have at least sixteen children. They were renowned as the best dancers in the land.

Tragedy struck Mikey when his young wife died while their daughter was very young. He sent his daughter to live with his wife's family in the Black Valley while he tended to his farm and visited her every three or four weeks, making the long journey by foot.

Inconsolable, he visited the Gaine's home each night. Unable to read or write, he had a deep love of Irish fairy stories and those of the Otherworld. One story he never tired of telling was of the night his mother died. Leaving a neighbour to sit by his mother in her last hours, Mikey went for a *walk up the road* in the early hours after nightfall. On the road, a stranger passed him; the person seemed to be headed for Mikey's house. When Mikey arrived home from his walk, the attendant told him there had been a visitor. Seemingly appearing from nowhere, the visitor walked in the front door, into the dying woman's bedroom, stayed for a moment or two and then departed into the night. As he recounted the story, Mikey always added his firm belief that the strange visitor was a long-deceased member of his mother's family, come to lead her safely Home.

Shortly before Mikey's wife died, she had been moved to a hospital in Killarney. Jim Gaine, an uncle of Tom, told of a hovering light that shone in a field near Mikey's house for a few nights before the young woman's passing. Mikey himself told how, after his arrival home from Killarney and on retiring to bed, he heard steps at the door, the sound of the latch being opened. In that instant, he knew his wife had died.

I was always intrigued with the stories Tom told of inexplicable lights he often saw in cabins which he knew were unoccupied at the time. On the night of his father's death, a light was seen hovering around the old home in Corrig, where Tom's father had been born.

In days of old, the Irish did not require any explanation to these strange phenomena. They lived out their daily lives with a complete acceptance of another world that, for centuries, filled their songs and their poems and their stories. Fact and fiction merged and infused their very being as inexorably as the air they breathed. From birth, a child's daily diet was made up as much of stories and music and song as mother's milk. It was unthinkable to enquire of a storyteller, *Is that true?* The spirit of the ancients was ingrained in their veins and fibre and marrow. It is a possible explanation of the older generations' down-to-earth application of their Catholic faith, a faith imbued with saints and angels, devils and witches and all things miraculous. It is the map of the Irish soul.

'And over there,' Tom said, 'that's where John Foley, my biggest fan, lived.'

I stopped and remembered with great affection my own connection with John.

John's mother died in 1930 before he was a year old. Tom's mother often visited the house with food and clothing for John's father, two sisters and brother. John lovingly declared that she was the only mother he knew and, many years later, asked Tom to say a special Mass for her each Mother's Day. In his youth, he much preferred running wild and carefree round the mountains than attending school. The school jester, he found it difficult keeping up with his peers; with so many children in the one classroom, it was easy for the teacher to pay him little heed.

Tom pointed, 'There's Mikey Batt's Hill.'

On their return from a fair in Kenmare, Tom and John, who were both in their early teens, had paused on a rock at the top of the hill. Perched high, John was throwing stones. He asked Tom what he would be when he grew up. Tom stood tall, glanced round; picked up a stone, strove to beat John. *I think I'll be a priest.*

John gulped, fell off the rock. *What! And miss out on all the fun with the girls!*

John migrated to Western Australia when he was 19 years old. He worked as a rouse-about for many years up North in various mining towns. He never married.

In 1985, shortly after the opening of the church in Girrawheen, John moved into the presbytery as the unofficial gardener. He was a special person, a simple man. We became great friends and more often than not he came to my home after Sunday Mass and stayed until after tea. Ever willing to help, he would do odd jobs for me, and loved to keep me in a plentiful supply of wood during the winter months. Always ready for a laugh, a lover of life and people, we enjoyed great moments of *cráic*.

Sadly, in 1999, he suffered a debilitating stroke which left him paralysed and unable to communicate verbally. He never lost the devilish glint in his blue eyes which lit up with glee when he recognised a visitor or filled with tears at sad news. In the immediate months following his stroke, I was not sure how cognisant he was, and wondered if he really knew who I was and the extent of his understanding. When Tom flew to Ireland following the death of his brother, Willie, in 2000, I visited John in the nursing home. His eyes lit up as usual. *Did he recognise me or was this just an automatic response?*

'I have sad news, John.' A cloud came in his eyes. 'Willie has died.'

The tears flowed. *My God,* I thought, *he does understand.*

John passed away four years later.

Ah, to be sure, as I looked over the fields towards the rundown cottage in which John was born so many years before, *isn't that John's spirit galloping through the heather!!*

At the fork of another unused road, Tom pointed to the place where a dancing platform had stood. Often after a hard day's work, particularly on a long summer's evening, the neighbours would congregate and dance: set dances, hornpipes and reels strained my ears. I was certain I could hear the mellow, haunting sound of a fiddle and *bodhrán,* the Irish drum that is held in the crook of one arm and rapped with the fingers of the other hand.

In other times, the surrounding mountains and valleys, the rivers and streams rang with the sound of men selling and buying cattle, women passing the time of day and children singing and frisking through the hills.

Today, the old glen is silent.

As we made our way home, the stillness and quietness and the ghosts of Lissyclerig – the many Gaines, Sullivans and Palmers – enveloped me.

Because of the poverty in Ireland, which resulted in the income of a lot of farms being insufficient to provide for a family, and very little work available away from the land, a considerable amount of young, marriageable girls either migrated or entered religious life. As a consequence, many of the farms could not be passed on when the men, who worked the fields on their own, died. Whilst outsiders have purchased some of the land, since Ireland joined the European Union in 1973, much of it has been taken over by the Forestry, the rest sliding into wasteland. The old house directly across the road from Tom's is now owned by an English couple who run a very successful bed and breakfast establishment.

As I was soon to discover, with the advent of Ireland into the EU and the subsequent boom in the Irish economy, the face of Old Ireland, to the older generation, is but a dim memory; to the technology-adept youth, it is the stuff of myth and fairy stories. In the years prior to the GFC, tourists in their thousands flocked to Ireland every summer with bulging wallets and vociferous demands to see Old Ireland. The pubs and eating-places rang with the sound of cash registers. Busloads of tourists choked the roads up and down the countryside. For a few short months, Old Ireland was taken from the closet, hosed down, dressed up, paraded for all and sundry; the glittering lights and camera flashes failed to see her weathered brow, her aged moans unheeded or ignored. With the shortening of the long summer evening, she was pushed back into the closet and sighed with relief.

The effects of the long flight and the *walk up the road* finally taking their toll, I strolled outside for a few moments before retiring. I bent my head back, marvelled at my first sighting of the strange Northern sky. As yet unaware of the existence of the Old Lady, and my ignorant complicity in her fate, I wrapped my arms around me to shield from the damp, night air and quivered with the added excitement of what I believed would be the culmination of a life-long quest: to find my roots, to locate my voice.

Conscious of the *presence* by my side, I turned towards the house and paused.

Tom was one of four brothers, of whom only John married. John and the youngest brother, Jimmy, migrated to America in their early years; John had no children. Tom entered the priesthood and Willy, the oldest, remained on the farm. Alone.

What will become of the old house, the now un-worked farmlands, in the years to come?

Perhaps they will re-unite with the ghosts of Lissyclerig.

Three

Lissyclerig, the townland in which Tom's home is situated, is about four kilometres north of the picturesque town of Kenmare, originally named *Nedeen – The Little Nest* – in south-west County Kerry. The town nestles at the mouth of the River Sheen that flows into Kenmare Bay, an estuary running inland from the sea at the foot of the Kerry and Cork Mountains. Linked with the internationally famous Ring of Kerry, which follows the northern coastline of the Iveragh Peninsula, with the rugged beauty of the south Ring of Beara, Kenmare is the perfect location from which to discover the South West of Ireland. Together with its many festivals, special weekends and events each year, the surrounding areas also offer an abundance of recreational activities: walking, fishing, mountain climbing, horse riding, golfing, river cruises and other sports. When asked by friends and acquaintances, before my departure from Australia, where I would be staying, many sighed, *Ah! Kerry! You're lucky – the most beautiful County in Ireland.* It did not take me long to appreciate their envy.

Washed by the Gulf Stream, Kerry enjoys a mild climate. In late May and June, most of the surrounding mountain land, woodlands, bogs and untenanted areas around the town of Kenmare abound with wildflowers: bluebells, cowslips, saxifrage, fair finger (wild foxgloves) and many wild orchids. Both the native Red Deer and the imported smaller Sika roam the surrounding mountains. In the nearby lonely and remote Black Valley, hooded crows, ravens and the rare clough can be spied in the rugged cliffs near the head of the valley.

Kenmare

A few days after my arrival, in the early evening, I went for a short stroll to the far grass patch at the back of Tom's house. A wild deer was quietly munching the grass. I was struck by its similar demeanour to the kangaroo. Tall and graceful, it stood quietly, looked deep into my eyes, evidently figured I was no danger and continued to munch.

During Tom's first holiday in Ireland after I started working with him, I was intrigued when I received a letter: on the back of the envelope was his address, Lissyclerig, Kenmare, Co. Kerry. Though surprised there was no house number or street name, I presumed Lissyclerig was the name of a holiday house for priests. Why else would it be named Lissyclerig if not for clerics!

On a lazy afternoon, some weeks after my arrival, I spent a fascinating couple of hours in Kenmare Library and learned the history of Irish townlands.

Ireland is sub-divided in a unique way: provinces into counties,

counties into baronies, baronies into parishes and parishes into townlands, the lowest-level, officially-defined geographical unit of land. After the partition of Ireland in 1921, what became the Republic of Ireland consists of three provinces: Leinster, Munster and Connacht. These are comprised of 26 counties. The province of Ulster in Northern Ireland has six counties.

There are over 62,000 townlands and they range in size from an acre or two up to many thousands of acres; the names of the majority indicate a Gaelic origin.

In pre-Christian Gaelic times, land was measured in terms of its economic potential rather than in fixed units of measurement: by the number of cattle that an area of pasture land could support or by the time taken to plough an area of arable land. It was common to allocate the land between streams as townlands. Where streams were not easily available, the townlands were delineated with clay and stone banks, which the Irish call ditches. Such apportionment of land was to well serve succeeding invaders of Ireland down the centuries.

With the success of the English King Henry II's invasion of Ireland in 1171, the Anglo-Normans conquered vast tracts of land and created more townlands. Following the Cromwellian conquest of Ireland at the beginning of the 1650s, the English Commonwealth Government was indebted to many private individual adventurers who had advanced sums of money to finance the war. The 1652 Act for the Settlement of Ireland provided for the confiscation and re-distribution of the lands of the defeated Irish, mostly Confederate Catholics, who had opposed Cromwell. Many soldiers who fought for Cromwell were owed large arrears of pay; they were re-paid by the granting of confiscated lands. Land was also to be provided to settlers from England and America following the conquest. To facilitate this extensive transfer of land, William Petty was appointed by Cromwell to measure and map the forfeited lands. Taking advantage of the ancient Gaelic configuration, he submitted the Down Survey, a map of Ireland based on ancient townlands, in just thirteen months.

The Composition Act of 1823 specified that tithes due to the Established Church, the Church of Ireland, which had hitherto been payable in kind, should now be paid in cash. Another valuation of the entire country, civil parish by civil parish, townland by townland, was carried out to determine how much each landholder had to pay. These tithes were fiercely resented by those who were not members of the Church of Ireland, particularly in the South where the majority were Catholic. Resentment also arose because of unjust exemptions from the tax, which produced spectacular inequalities. In Munster, for example, tithes were payable on potato patches but not on grassland, with the result that the poorest had to pay most. To compensate for the loss of income following the Tithe War in 1831, local Church of Ireland clergymen were required to produce lists of those liable for the tithes and who had not paid. This was a relatively easy task since townland registers recorded each tithe defaulter.

Impressed by the accuracy of the division of land and how these ancient allotments facilitated the speed in which surveys were accomplished, I continued my exploration.

In the immediate years after the Great Famine of 1845 to 1847, under the guidance of Richard Griffith, another survey of Irish property ownership was conducted. The Tenement Act of 1842 provided for a uniform valuation of all property, to be based on the productive capacity of land and the potential rent of buildings. The valuation was arranged by county, barony, poor law union, civil parish and townland. Results of the survey were used to determine the amount of tax each person had to pay towards the support of the famine victims within each poor law union.

The valuation was never intended as a census substitute. However, as most polls were destroyed after the famine, Griffith's Valuation, available today, in major libraries, can be used as an excellent census alternative and provides the only detailed guide to where people lived in the mid nineteenth century and what property they possessed.

Given the common use of some surnames, families are often identified by the townland in which they live; often these names are the only records which survive of the families who held the land in pre-plantation times. *Bally* or *Baile*, which both mean 'home', are usually compounded with personal or family names and examples can be found all over Ireland as in Ballywalter, Ballyjamesduff, Ballyrussle.

The townland name continues to be one of the more important divisions in the Irish postal system, although this role has now been replaced in urban areas – and in most areas of Northern Ireland – by road names. However, I was interested to learn that the Northern Ireland Assembly passed a motion in 2001 requesting all Government departments make use of townland addresses in their correspondence and publications.

During the last, dark years before the Treaty that gave birth to the present Republic of Ireland, two Gaine families, which included Tom's grandfather, were evicted from their land in Corrig, a townland adjacent to Lisslyclerig, by the agent for Lord Lansdowne, the absentee landowner of much of the land surrounding Kenmare. When forced to retire from the Dublin Metropolitan Police under Article X of the Treaty that separated the south and north of Ireland, Tom's father – himself a Tom – returned to Kenmare in 1923 and, at the age of 44, bought the small farm at Lyssyclerig with his meagre savings.

The Gaines returned to their homeland.

Tired, yet excited at what I had learned, I bundled all the notes I had made and references for further investigation and set off back to Lyssyclerig. Not to a holiday house for clerics, but to the cottage and land in which Tom was born – the native soil that had nourished and nurtured him, that played a large part in the development of his deep and abiding love for all of creation.

Four

With Tom attending to business, I was pleased to have a day to myself. Tourist book in hand, a pack on my back, I walked the four kilometres to Kenmare; it is an easy feat – no pun intended! – it is all down-hill. My first stop was the Tourist/Heritage Centre, where I purchased a map of the town.

Twice awarded Tidiest Town of the Year, the two main thoroughfares, Henry and Main Street, cross each other in a large X, although the top half is wider than the bottom. The road that joins the lower half is called The Square, opposite a lovely park. Joining the widest top half of the crossed main roads is Shelbourne Street.

Despite its cosmopolitan atmosphere, with an abundance of gourmet restaurants and A class hotels, health shops and delicatessens, bustling tourist shops in which there was an amazing range of local crafts, pottery, Celtic jewellery, kitsch souvenirs such as leprechauns and shamrock emblems, and the tens of thousands of international visitors during the summer months, the town's traditional culture survived. The shop and hotel fronts were painted in vivid primary colours, as were the houses situated in the off-streets of the town; a visual delight I was to experience all around Ireland's towns.

I was thrilled to discover it was Market Day, the most important day of the month, which, I was to learn, was held in neighbouring towns on succeeding weekends. Loud sounds of gossip and haggling reverberated on the streets surrounding the park as the local farmers strove to get the best price for their livestock: sheep, goats, cows whose own voices competed with their owners'.

'Ah, and haven't ye got a good deal there, Michael? The missus, she warned me to be careful of ye.'

'And where'd we all be without a good missus behind us? Aye, happy I am with the price now.'

With that, the two men sealed the bargain with the age old custom: they both spat in their right hand and, with a nod of the head, shook hands.

On both sides of The Square, curb-side stalls groaned with local produce, as well as fish and gastronomical delights such as herbed feta, pickled salmon, a wide variety of olives and other delicacies I had not expected to see in a small Irish town.

It was to take some time for me to appreciate the difference in the population dispersal between Ireland and Australia. Like most Australians, I lived in a sprawling suburban environment that stretched out in all directions from the main city areas. Country towns are sparse and often many, many kilometres apart. I usually only visited a non-urban town when driving from one city to another. Whilst I loved to spend some hours on the weekend at a suburban market, I had never enjoyed that experience in an Australian country town.

Besides the food stalls, there were others that offered a wide variety of beautiful woven rugs, intricately knitted jumpers and other items of clothing and bric-a-brac. My eye was caught by a particular rug which I thought would look lovely in Tom's newly-built sun-room, a possible 'thank you' gift for his hospitality.

I knew I would return on next month's market day.

A short walk from the centre of town is Cromwell's Bridge, an arch-shaped stone bridge built without mortar. Yet again, this was something to amaze me constantly during my travels: the ancients' ability to build forts, bridges, walls with stone that was cut and fitted so perfectly, without any cement or mortar, some of them thousands of years old. Although his armies conquered the O'Sullivan Beare holdings to the east of Kenmare, Oliver Cromwell never came to the town. The name is derived, instead, from the Irish *crombheal,* 'moustache', referring to its shape. In ancient times, the bridge was used by the Franciscan Monks at a nearby monastery to enjoy a dip in the nearby waters of Our Lady's Well, set in a lush, multi-treed hollow, a statue of the Virgin Mary nestled in a rock face.

Our Lady's Well

A survey conducted in the mid-1900s claimed there were as many as 3,000 holy wells in Ireland. A visit offers an opportunity to witness sacred sites and to participate in rituals that have continued, in various forms, since the time of the Druids. Where once a sacrifice may have taken place, today a bride might look into the waters for inspiration or good luck; a cripple might bathe in the waters and have faith in its curative powers.

My fascination with Celtic mythology and spirituality was born many years prior to my visit. During the late 1980s and early 1990s, I belonged to a women's spirituality group made up of many Irish friends. We devoured the ancient beliefs and practices with a passion, often creating our own versions of Celtic rituals to celebrate special moments in our lives.

In their religious belief and practice, the earth-centred Celts – a grain-cultivating, cattle-raising people – emphasised cyclic regeneration as opposed to a linear movement upwards. One of the features of Irish Celtic cosmogony was the power of place. Their gods and goddesses were not remote beings who lived in a far-off heaven. They were magical people who lived in a parallel dimension, located under the earth, hidden in a mound, beneath the sea, on a plain clouded in mist or in the waters of a holy well. The Celtic Otherworld, called *Tir na nO'g*, the 'land of the young', was both the place of the dead and the land of eternal youth. Inhabitants from the land of faerie found it easy to pass between two worlds; whilst there are tales of mortals finding secret doorways to this Otherworld, their return to the physical world was impossible. From sources in *Tir na nO'g*, water flowed into the physical world to fill springs or gush forth as rivers such as the Boyne and the Shannon. To visit a Sacred Place and drink from the holy waters or to bathe in them would bestow the power of the gods and goddesses in the form of poetic inspiration, wisdom and healing.

The residents of *Tir na nO'g* were seen as allies. There were river guardians whose help the ancients sought with fishing and safe passage; forest guardians and plant spirits assisted when asked for healing and other magical matters. When a Celt called upon a god or goddess for help, he or she would look for signs that the request had been granted: if an animal appeared at that time, it was of great significance. The person who asked for help would look to the characteristics of the animal to determine what lessons it had to give with regard to the request. If the animal led to a solution or pointed to a particular way forward, it would then be linked to the god or goddess who had been summoned. The next time that archetype was drawn or sculptured, the animal helper would be included in the image. This connectedness was fundamental to the Celtic world view. Be it a stone, an animal, an archetype, a plant, a sunset or a cloud – all were linked.

A well-known inhabitant of the land of faerie is the *bean sí*, or Banshee, a female faerie who attached herself to certain families and let out a groaning cry at the death of a family member; the elves, a green-clad folk who loved hunting and riding; the water-dweller mermaids with human upper bodies and tails of fish; the subterranean sprites, or gnomes, who jealously guarded all Earth's treasures. And of course, the loveable symbolic, much used – much abused – leprechaun: a brown-faced, shaggy-haired, brown-clothed, three-foot pixie who helped mortals with their work and completed jobs around the house whilst its occupants slept.

The people visited the wells at special times of the year: *Samain, Imbolc, Bealtaine* and *Lughnasa* celebrated on the first day of November, February, May and August respectively. *Samhain*, the most important annual Festival, the beginning of the Celtic New Year which we now celebrate as Halloween, was a special magical time when the people made sacrifice to the gods in the hope of good fortune for the New Year. The veil between the living and the dead was at its thinnest point where visions of 'the good people' were often seen. The important festival of *Bealtime* marked the beginning of the warm weather, when the cattle could be driven out to open grazing after months spent in confined sheds. The Druids' peat fires were lit and the cattle herded between two such fires to protect them against disease. Feasting and dancing followed. May Day has remained a time of celebration.

A Sacred Place consisted of three elements: the well, spring or other water source, a sacred tree, usually very large and old, and a hill or standing stone. These features played a vital part in the prescribed rituals or *patterns*. The participants rubbed the standing stone (and later day statue) for a special blessing; the sick tied a strip of cloth, or *clootie*, to the holy tree after they washed, bathed or drank from the well. As the rag rotted, so did the owner's illness.

Clooties

Many Sacred Places included a large stone with a depression. Those large enough to hold a person were called *beds*: women would lie on such stones to ensure conception. *Patterns* included a circular walk, always completed in the same direction in which the sun travelled.

Supernatural fish, especially salmon or trout, appeared in a well's depths to those seeking omens for the future. The salmon were credited with being bearers of *iomas*, the 'light that illumines', the insight and wisdom that comes from a supernatural encounter, rather than the knowledge acquired through conventional study.

Isolated from the influence of the Roman Empire, after Patrick, Irish Christianity evolved differently from most of its European counterparts. The people happily wove much of their Old Religion into the New, even though the lyric phenomena associated with the Celtic wells, and indeed all aspects of Celtic spirituality, was revalorized in terms and by symbols universally understood in Christianity. In a crossing of the boundary between the two cultures, the pagan tree took on the symbol of the Cross, and the wells of the pagan *Brighid*, the Otherworld Goddess/Queen of fertility and healing, who was re-incarnated as St. Brigid, were re-named Lady Wells. Another crossover symbol was the fish. The sacred trout or salmon evolved into a Christian saint after whom the particular well was re-named. Christian saints substituted for other beings of the land of faerie were believed to hold almost exactly the same powers as their pagan forebears.

Christian churches were often built near the pagan wells, and the early Celtic Church used them for baptism. Eventually, these were replaced by a font in the building. A number of old churches contain a crypt or grotto that opens into a subterranean spring: a Sacred Place, close to earth and water, the innermost sanctum, the hidden holy centre.

In the ensuing centuries after Patrick, as Catholicism took a firm hold, the holy wells remained important focal points for the practice of folk-religion, especially when Catholic worship was forbidden during the infamous Penal Laws in the years 1621-1829. Though universal Christian practice gradually eroded much of the Church's earlier Celtic influence, such inheritance continues to be evident in some of the beliefs and practices of the people today. The practice of circumambulation – walking round and round sacred sites – is an important ritual.

This is particularly seen among the Traveller Community, Ireland's gypsies. During a library visit, I read a charming essay written by a primary school girl from Co. Wexford who told how her family goes 'to Holy Wells in the summer and in the winter. God blesses Holy Wells and the water cures people. My sister's hair began to fall out. She went to St. Kevin's Well and now her hair is all grown back'.

Each year, on 15 August, the Feast of the Assumption – an important date in Kenmare – pilgrims congregate at Our Lady's Well for Mass, an event I happily looked forward to. At other times, it is a meeting place for the Stations of the Cross.

After I descended Cromwell's Bridge and entered the rock-speckled grotto, I rubbed my hand across the Lady's feet. I gazed up, noted the position of the sun and began a slow walk around the perimeter of the Sacred Place, offered a silent prayer of praise to all the gods and goddesses of both heaven and earth in thanksgiving for the opportunity to connect with my cultural and religious ancestors.

I retraced my steps over the bridge and took another path, this time, to Druid's Circle. Set in a riverside glade, on the banks of the River Finnihy, it is the largest stone-circle in the south-west of Ireland. Built around 1000BC for ritual and ceremonial purposes, it comprises fifteen large stones in a 17 metre diameter circle with a larger burial boulder in the centre. Each stone is over a metre in height and width.

The name 'Druid's Circle' is a misnomer.

Ireland is often thought of, even today, as a Celtic country. Yet the Celts, when they first arrived from Europe around 400 BC, were invaders. Ireland was first inhabited around 7500 BC by settlers who probably came from Scotland to what is now Co. Antrim in the North. These early Mesolithic (Middle Stone Age) people were primitive hunters and fishermen. They settled the coasts and the bigger river valleys, especially in the northern half of the island, although archaeological remains of their settlements have been found as far south as Co. Cork. They were joined by a new wave of settlers around 3500 BC, a group now known as Neolithic (New Stone Age). The new arrivals' ability to cultivate land enabled them to outstrip the hunter-gatherers and to establish permanent settlements. Their coming marked the beginning of civilised life in Ireland.

These ancient people celebrated life and death in stone. Neolithic burial sites testify to the supreme importance they attached to funerary ritual. They range from stone circles, as seen in Kenmare, and dolmens – two or three standing stones supporting a huge capstone – to the passage graves of which those in the Boyne Valley in Co. Meath, north of Dublin, are, from what I have been told, the most spectacular and which include Newgrange, the most celebrated of all and one of the wonders of prehistoric Europe.

Undoubtedly, on their arrival in Ireland, the Celts, who brought the Iron Age with them, took advantage of the extraordinary craftsmanship of the people they invaded. They regarded the megalithic monuments with a transparent sense of awe and added their own unique art form. Although little evidence remains to shed light on how the Celts buried their dead, according to Celtic lore Newgrange is the burial place of the legendary Celtic Kings of Tara as well as the residence of *Dagda*, the father of the gods. Also known as *Eochaid Ollathair*, *Dagda* was the leader of the mythological ancients of Ireland, the *Tuatha Dé Danann*, and was credited with many powers. He possessed a cauldron that was never empty, fruit trees that always bore fruit, and two boars, one living and one perpetually roasting on a spit. He owned a harp that automatically played to summon the seasons and a magical club that could not only kill men, but also bring them back to life. His son, *Oenghus*, was the god of love.

At the festival of Samhain, the time of changes, Oenghus went to the Dagda and begged him to grant him the tenancy of Brug na Bóinne for the space of a night and a day. The Dagda gazed fondly on his son and readily agreed to yield up his palace on those terms. He departed immediately, and for the space of a night and a day, Oenghus held the kingship of the fairy mound.

At the end of the allotted time, the Dagda came again to Brug na Bóinne and requested the return of his palace. But Oenghus refused his father, explaining that he was the rightful owner of the mound. He had been granted lordship over it for a night and a day, and since the passage of time consists of nothing more than a night and a day, following each other in endless succession, he was now master of the place of all eternity.

The Dagda realized he had been tricked. He went away, taking his household and his people with him, leaving Oenghus to enjoy Goibhnui's ale and the feast that never failed.

Seduced by the silence, I sat on the grassy mound of the Circle which, I reasoned, should rightly be re-named the Neolithic Circle. My imagination swam with images of a Stone Age people, their backs bent to the Atlantic wind as they built their circle of stone, their chants almost drowned by the gurgle of the nearby brook and a lone cuckoo. I pondered on the plight of these ancient people who were taken over by the Celts, a people of whom we know so little. A people who built the wonders in the Valley of the Kings: Dowth, Knowth and Newgrange. A people who definitely were not just simple farmers.

With a deep cognisance that I would return, I headed back to town.

I checked my map and crossed The Square to the house originally occupied by Sister Francis Clare Cusack, the Nun of Kenmare. As I stood beside the wrought-iron gate, I recalled an article I had written in 2003 about this remarkable woman.

Margaret Cusack was born in Dublin on 6 May, 1829; her parents were descended from the landed gentry, devout members of the Episcopalian faith.

The tireless work of her father, Dr. Samuel Cusack, at a dispensary north of Dublin and his willingness to attend to the poorest women in their homes during the long hours of giving birth, left a lasting impression on his daughter, coupled with a deep sense of justice.

At the age of twenty-two, following the death of her father and that of her fiancé, she entered an Anglican Convent in London. A weak heart prevented her dream of joining Florence Nightingale. With the vast poverty and wretchedness in London, she believed there would be ample opportunity to work for the alleviation of human suffering. Again, disappointment dogged her. A rule which she found particularly difficult was one which prohibited the Sisters from doing anything more than reading prayers to the sick poor.

After years of prayer, deep thought and study, in particular the works of John Henry Newman and his fellow founders of the Oxford Movement, together with an increased disillusionment with the Anglican Church in general, Margaret turned to the Church of Rome. She found some answers, and to the chagrin of her family, was received into the Catholic Church on 2 July, 1858. The cardinal who received her extracted a promise that she would dedicate her life to writing Catholic literature. The keeping of such promise was to bring her both love and disdain. Little did she know, that after joining the Order of Poor Clare's under the name of Sr. Francis Clare in Newry, Ireland in 1859, her pen would be a powerful weapon in staving off starvation for many of West Ireland's poor. After boldly exposing the roots of famine in Ireland, including landlordism and governmental tyranny, her compassion and solidarity with the destitute would lead to two threats upon her life.

In October, 1861, at the invitation of the parish priest, together with three other sisters, she made the arduous trek south to what they could only describe as the most utter desolation and despair of Kerry's needy. Their mission was to open a convent in Kenmare

In the beginning of her literary life, her writings, in the main, were confined to history books and publications rooted in the Catholic Faith. As the head of Kenmare publications – a feat achieved more than one hundred years before women were accepted as CEOs of business enterprises – the income from the 50 plus books she wrote financed the Order and its many charitable works. In 1868 she published her *Illustrated History of Ireland*, a monumental piece that attracted the acclamation of high-ranking church and state leaders on both sides of the Atlantic. The Archbishop of Cincinnati declared it 'the only Irish history worthy of its name', and John Mitchel from the *Irish Citizen* of Dublin, proclaimed that 'a woman had accomplished what men had failed to do'.

After her successful use of the press as a pulpit to teach religion and patriotism, Francis Clare turned her considerable talent in writing to address social reform, indicating in her writing ways to alleviate the causes of stress and distress which led to war. She vigorously supported the people of Kenmare who figured prominently in the old days of the Land League and the later Home Rule Movement. Protestant residents enthusiastically joined with their Catholic neighbours during the progress of these movements.

Whilst originally pleased with her writings on Catholic doctrine, the ecclesiastical authorities turned against her, as so often happens in the Church to women who take on a leading role. The Nun of Kenmare, the *Voice of the Voiceless*, was branded an agitator: she dared to rock the Establishment in which, it could be said, the Church had an interest. Archbishop McCabe of Dublin issued an edict forbidding women to take part in politics. He raised the question of whether the whole country was seeking refuge under women's petticoats!

On 10 December, 1880, a vast crowd of men and women marched from Killarney, about 32 kilometres north of Kenmare, to assemble at the Convent gate. They came to show their support of their beloved Nun of Kenmare and their horror and indignation at two anonymous assassination threats she had received.

In 1881, circumstances so contrived against her that she was forced to leave Kenmare. Jealousy and calumny continued to thwart her every move. She eventually left Ireland for the New World.

Heartbroken by what she saw as betrayal by many of the Catholic clergy, the leaders of the Church to which she had converted her allegiance as a young woman, she returned to England and sought refuge with family and friends in the faith into which she was baptised. The Nun of Kenmare, the *Voice of the Voiceless,* passed away on Monday 5 June, 1899.

For the second time that day, I paused. And prayed. I offered thanks and praise for a woman, so dear to my own heart and to countless others, both male and female, who spent their lives in an attempt to alleviate the suffering of the dispossessed. To the equally countless people who, in my own time, refuse to accept that the bounty of our beautiful world is only for the rich; to men and women whose lives are steeped in the concrete belief that all people are equal.

I re-crossed the Square and ascended the stairs that lead off the Tourist/Heritage Centre, to the Kenmare Lace Museum. I spent a lazy hour inspecting the intricate displays and, fascinated, watched the woman on duty ply her needle. As she worked, she filled me in on the history of Kenmare Lace.

When Sr. Clare and the few Sisters with her arrived in Kenmare, the building of the convent and church provided several years of much needed employment for local tradesmen and labourers struggling to overcome the devastation of the Great Famine. In recognition of the lack of remunerative employment for women, the Sisters, under the leadership of Mother Abbess O'Hagan, opened an industrial school which provided opportunities for the local women to learn skills that would help them both at home and to find employment in the New World to which many were forced to migrate. They were taught the craft of lace making and, due to the unique patterns, the world-famous Kenmare Lace was born.

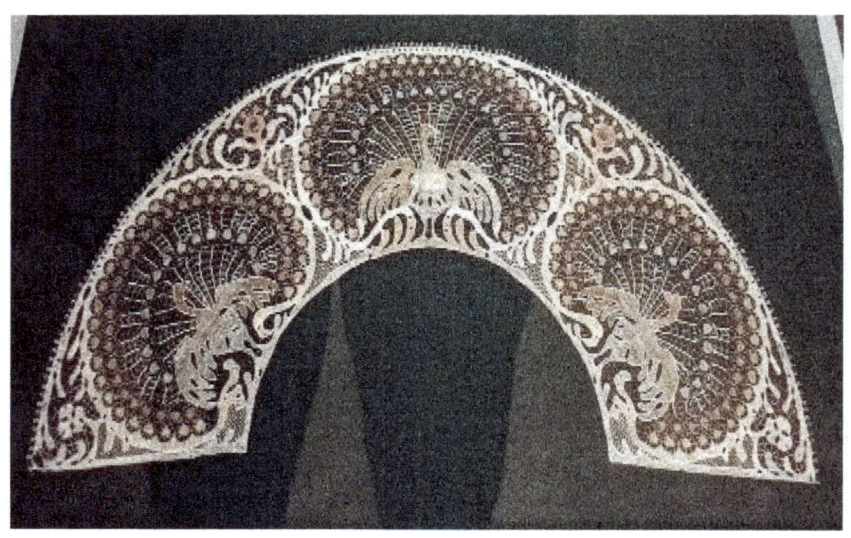

Kenmare Lace
This Photo ***by Unknown Author is licensed under*** CC BY-SA

The girls, simple and uneducated, came from rural families. Understandably, much of the early work was spoiled and soiled but gradually, through patience and encouragement, the products began to improve to such an extent that many girls were capable of earning from five to eighteen shillings a week, a considerable wage at that time. By 1869, sales figures had reached 500 pounds per annum and the making of needlepoint lace began. Although only Irish crochet had been produced up until this time, it was so skilfully worked that it became known as 'Point d'Irelandaise' and could be bought in Paris and London. Wealthy tourists who travelled along the 'Prince of Wales Route' from Killarney to Glengarriff in Co. Cork were encouraged to stop at the convent to view and purchase some lace whilst four fresh horses were harnessed for the continuation of the journey. On her visit to the region, Queen Victoria, an admirer of the fine lace patterns, bought five pieces.

Samples were submitted to the Cork Exhibition of 1883. Such

was the acclaim of the work that the Art Department at Kensington in London sent a lace expert to further the education provided by the nuns. Art classes were added to the curriculum under the tutelage of James Brennan, the Headmaster of the Science and Art School in Cork City. Both the young male art students and the female lace makers distinguished themselves with medals and prizes awarded them in competitions with all the art schools of Great Britain.

The young boys were not neglected. They were given lessons in drawing and design and trained in leatherwork and woodcarving in which Celtic ornamentation was freely used.

As the school's fame widened, the Irish Education Department stepped in and paid the school according to results. The money received was used to improve facilities and the nuns purchased the most sophisticated tools and equipment available. A new spacious, well-lit room was erected for the lace workers, with a kindergarten attached. As well as the increasing orders for lace placed by English patrons, the school's fame attracted buyers from the New World. In 1886, Mrs. Winacles, the wife of an American millionaire, commissioned a bedcover which fetched the astronomical sum of £300. Teachers who had obtained their Art Certificates from Kenmare were readily employed in England, some of them appointed 'Specialist Teachers of Drawing' in many London schools.

With the changes brought about by the 1914-18 war, the market for lace declined and the workers emigrated, mainly to England, the United States and Australia, taking their skills with them. Despite this setback, the fame of Kenmare Lace never died. Queen Elizabeth II received an antique bed-cover of Kenmare needlepoint among her wedding gifts. The Vatican has a needlepoint rochet – a white vestment generally worn by Anglican and Catholic bishops in choir work – designed in Kenmare and an embroidered mitre was presented to Pope John Paul II in 1980. The lace room with its display of antique and modern lace is still visited today by hundreds of tourists. The women who staff the display continue to work the lace and in recent years, Kenmare lace has experienced a renaissance.

Before leaving the museum, I perused the offerings on sale and purchased an exquisite lace collar. A gift for one of my daughters, perhaps?

Sated, for the time being, by what I had seen in my walk through the ages, yet eager to learn more, I headed to the Kenmare Library. Anxious to use the library card I had previously borrowed from Tom, I was disappointed to find it closed. I looked around to find out when it would be open. On a notice board opposite the front door of the Library, as well as finding its opening hours, I read a large sign:

Do not place returns in this slot when library closed.

I glanced behind, saw the slot in the door. Over this was another sign:

Place returns in this slot when library closed.

I smiled. Ah, the ways of the Irish.

I walked back to the Post Office. Although I had taken some photos during my stroll, I am not the greatest photographer and I was keen to buy some postcards of the Well and the Druid's Circle. As well as the Post Office, there are, as mentioned, many tourist shops down Henry Street. I eventually found what I wanted and then plonked myself at a table outside the Wander Inn, one of the many pubs, and ordered a pint. I watched the world pass by.

Ireland, a much respected and, in those years, a wealthy partner of the European Union, was a favourite destination for countless young Europeans who flocked there each year for summer work. In the summer months, tourists from all over the world descended in their thousands. There were also many refugees from the world's trouble spots. Unlike the way refugees are incarcerated in hot, desperate, remote prisons in Australia and elsewhere whilst they await processing, in Ireland they were housed in the local communities. Just outside of town, on the way to Lissyclerig, an old hotel had been converted into a residence where they lived whilst waiting for their visas. They were free to go to town to do their shopping.

As I imbibed my Guinness, the babble of diverse languages quickly drowned the ancient chants.

A woman with a broad Scottish accent asked if she could sit at my table. With rapid fire, she regaled me with her story. A Norwegian, who spoke ten languages, married to a Scot who had died twelve months previously, she now spent her time travelling on her own around all of Europe. An hour and another pint later, I executed a retreat.

Before my attempt to walk back to Lissyclerig – up-hill this time – I decided to pay another visit to Druid's Circle. The lazy, early-evening laughter of the brook grounded me. A lone cuckoo sang into the silence. *Amazing*, I pondered. *That's just how the bird sounds: cook-oo, cook-oo.*

A far cry from the Kookaburra's laugh.

In the early time, the Wongaibon people were not content. Though there were springs of water and an interesting supply of food, the land was hazy and dark. The sun and the moon were together high in the sky but shrouded in mist. The people longed for more light and warmth.

The Creator separated the sun and the moon and created certain periods of darkness which He called night followed by a period He called day. The Wongaibon people watched with pleasure as the first day dawned. They were happy.

But they began to take it for granted. This surprised and disappointed the Creator. He had expected that they would arise each morning, happy yet again to enjoy and appreciate each new dawn.

After trying many things – he made each new day ablaze with colour – he decided to create a rare and special bird, one that had the power to actually wake and emotionally stir these seemingly, dull, uninterested people.

The bird was indeed a magnificent looking creature with strong wings and bright, piercing eyes. Its call was loud and raucous. It echoed over and over again in the still, quiet world, sounding just like wild human laughter.

As dawn was breaking the very next day, the Creator sent his new bird out into the world. He told the bird to let his rollicking, loud laugh echo across the Western Plains until every Wongaibon man, woman and child woke up.

As programmed, the bird did his job extremely well. As the sun's first rays touched the dark night sky, his hoots of laughter shattered the silence of the dawn. The sound certainly did disturb the people as they had never been disturbed before. It was amazing! It was astonishing!

At first, the Wongaibon people rubbed their eyes lazily and longed to go back to sleep. Soon, however, they found that they actually began to feel better, brighter and healthier because of rising early. They began to appreciate the wonder of daybreak, the special coolness of the breeze and the mystical, marvellous beauty of the sky. They also seemed to be more aware of all the other wonders of the world.

A mate was created for the bird and many chicks were hatched. Soon, a vast army of birds was spreading its loud, celebratory message of joy right across the land each and every morning.

The Creator was very happy with his kookaburra.

– The Wongaibon People
North Western New South Wales
Laugh Kookaburra Laugh, Jean A. Ellis

My maternal grandmother and I were very close. She loved to tell me stories.

'Elizabeth,' she said many times, 'whenever you hear a kookaburra laugh you know it will rain within 24 hours.'

Down the years, it has appeared to me that she was right – most of the time.

I rose, bowed to the ancients in this land of my ancestors. Bid my farewell. An ancient chant flooded my imagination, wrapped me in comfort. I turned towards Lissyclerig. Halted.

The chant. One of comfort? Or challenge?

Could I – did I – hear the voice of the ancients of the land of my birth?

Druid's Circle, Kenmare

Five

Wednesday 2 June, was the 47th Anniversary of Tom's Ordination. We went to 10 am Mass in Kenmare and then drove to Killarney for lunch. Tom usually goes to Killarney at least once a week for shopping.

Killarney staggered me. Of course, I had never experienced such scale of the tourist industry. There are literally hundreds of hotels, huge buildings all built in old English style, guest houses and Bed and Breakfast accommodation. A mecca for tourists in Co. Kerry, Killarney is a city renowned for its splendid scenery, in particular its lakes. The three lakes are contained within Killarney National Park. My guide book stresses that 'although the landscape is dotted with castles and abbeys, the lakes are the focus of attention: the moody watery scenery is subject to subtle shifts of light and colour'.

Killarney Lakes
This Photo by Unknown Author is licensed under CC BY

The smallest lake is the Upper Lake, south-west of Killarney. It flows into the second , Muckross Lake, via the Long Range River. The Meeting of the Waters is a beauty spot, best seen from Dinis Island, in which the two smaller lakes meet Lough Leane, the largest of which lies closest to Killarney. Lough Leane is dotted with uninhabited islands and fringed with wooded slopes.

To the south-west of Killarney, between Lough Leane and Upper Lake is a beautiful range of mountains of which Purple Mountain is the highest at 832 metres. The area provides amazing walking and cycling tracks that weave through the mountains and around the lakes.

We visited Muckross House, the 19th century manor of Lord Vincent, Lord Kenmare's neighbour. It is now a museum and heritage centre. A magnificent building, it commands an unbelievably striking panorama of Lough Leane. Not far from Muckross House are the ruins of Muckross Abbey which was founded by the Franciscans in 1448 and burnt down by Cromwell in 1653. A little further north, again beside Lough Leane, is Ross Castle, built around 1420, which was the last stronghold under Irish control to be taken by Cromwell's forces.

We had a special celebratory meal at the Lord Kenmare Hotel. Ireland's crystal clear rivers and streams, and the seas which surround the county have always been a rich source of food. Whether it be salmon, the king of fish, or the humble herring, the noble oyster or the simple cockle, there has always been an abundant supply to be had for the fishing or the taking. I was determined, during my stay in Ireland, to take advantage of the plentiful opportunities to dine on my favourite salmon. Despite the wide variety of meals from different lands on the menu, we stuck to a traditional Irish meal. We started with a rich leek and potato soup. Well do I remember the thick, rich soups my mother used to make, soups that were most certainly of the *'aten and drinken'* style. This was followed by a dish of steamed mussels in a full-bodied white wine sauce. The main course was grilled salmon in herb butter and a large bowl of hot roasted root vegetables and creamy colcannon, another favourite of mine: mashed potato and cabbage and chives all mixed together. And could we not finish our festive meal in one of the grandest hotels in the grandest city of Co. Kerry with anything other than a mouth-watering apple pie?

> *God be with the happy times,*
> *When the troubles we had not*
> *And our mothers made colcannon,*
> *In the three-legged pot.*
>
> *Traditional Rhyme*

We then went to see a show at The Laurels Hotel by Liam O'Connor. He has done to Irish music what Michael Flatley did to Irish dance. Liam plays the button accordion and can he make it sing! There were other musicians, a singer and two dancers. I could not resist the temptation: I rose and went to the back of the auditorium, gyrated and danced with the music in the aisle. A woman next to me asked: 'Are you the choreographer?'

Liam was booked to play at the hotel for five nights a week for five months! The auditorium would hold at least 500 people. Most of the patrons were middle-aged and older tourists; packed buses pull into Killarney every night. Liam O'Connor's concert was just one of many. I was gob-smacked by the number of tourists everywhere we travelled. Most of them were American.

I had heard and read about the *Celtic Tiger* some years prior to my visit without really knowing what it meant. The first recorded use of the phrase was used in a 1994 report by Kevin Gardiner, from the Morgan Stanley global financial service in New York. The term referred to Ireland's similarity to the *East Asian Tigers* of South Korea, Singapore, Hong Kong and Taiwan. The rapid economic growth in Ireland during the 1990s – at times referred to as 'The

Boom' or 'Ireland's Economic Miracle' – transformed it from one of Europe's poorer countries into one of its wealthiest. Whilst I am no economist, I have read that the causes of Ireland's growth in those years are the subject of some debate, but credit was primarily given to state-driven economic development: social partnership between employers, government and unions, increased participation in the labour force of women, decades of investment in domestic higher education; targeting of foreign direct investment; a low corporation tax rate; an English-speaking workforce, and crucial EU membership – which provided transfer payments and export access to the Single Market. Together with this, I presumed, must be added the lessening of sectarian and other violence resulting in a more 'tourist friendly' environment. Ah, to be sure and ain't I now much wiser? Does that make it easier for me to comprehend the present down-turn in the Irish economy? Not really.

In the mid-90s, Michael Flatley choreographed a show called *The Celtic Tiger*. In an interview, he said: 'The Celtic Tiger portrays the oppression of a people. The tiger itself symbolizes the awakening of their spirit in the struggle for freedom.'

Night fell as we drove home to Kenmare along the mountain road. About half way between Killarney and Moll's Gap – the gap in the mountain ranges from which one drives down into Kenmare – there is a plateau and about half a kilometre of long, straight road. This plateau is quite high in the mountains and there is a very large lake there. I couldn't get over the number of sheep asleep on this stretch of road. Tom said they go on to the road because it is warmer than the damp grass. Evidently, everyone is used to it – rare it is that any sheep get killed.

It was a special night. Down the years, we used to always celebrate his anniversary. 'Twas nice, indeed, to do it again after such a long time.

Two days later, we went back to Killarney, this time to celebrate the 78th birthday of Peggy Gaine, Tom's cousin. Peggy, who is half blind, lives in Corrig, the neighbouring townland to Lissyclerig, on the Kenmare-Killarney Road, about a fifteen minute drive from Tom's home. Her house is about a five minute drive to Moll's Gap. Peggy's father and Tom's father were brothers. Peggy never married and, except for a few years in Dublin when she was younger, she has always lived in Corrig. She returned to Corrig to look after her bachelor brother, John, when their parents died. Tom and Peggy are the sole remaining direct members of that branch of the Gaine family. Tom drives Peggy to Killarney when she wants to do some shopping.

We shopped a little, and then had a birthday meal in the Hotel Europe, a five-star hotel with stunning views of the Killarney lakes and mountains. Although the large hotels are very grand, I prefer the smaller ones. This is no derision of the large hotels; I prefer the ambience of the small 'pub-like' atmosphere. But a celebration is a celebration. During our lunch, I asked Peggy why she had never travelled to Australia. She raised her head and a look of utter amazement spread across her face.

'Australia! I would never go to Australia. People get eaten by sharks in Australia!'

I dared not debate, but did smile to myself as I recalled an article in a newspaper I had read a few days prior to our trip to Killarney of a person being attacked by an enormous squid in the sea off the west coast of North West Ireland.

Tom and Peggy had a weekly Sunday routine: Tom joined Peggy for lunch which, though nearly blind, Peggy cooked; more often than not, a baked dinner. After lunch, they watched either a football or hurling match on the television.

After lunch during my first participation in this weekly routine, I sat with them for about fifteen minutes and desperately tried to engage myself with the game on the TV. I excused myself and went for a 90 minute walk *up the road*. Yes, I was indeed very lucky to be in Kerry. One mountain rolls into another, seemingly endless. They change face rapidly; one moment they are green pastures, the next, craggy and barren. The sheep do not seem to mind what type of ground they grazed and galloped along. Whilst no expert on sheep, they seemed to me to be like what I imagined mountain goats are – very quick-footed. As I strode up the winding Killarney Road towards Moll's Gap, I enjoyed my own ritual: I embraced the silence, allowed it to penetrate my whole being. The *presence* was with me, beside me, around me. I was at complete peace.

Road to Moll's Gap

On my arrival back at Peggy's home, the match was over. We had a quick hot drink and Tom drove an alternative route home through the most beautiful valley. What can I say about this valley? Desolate, lonely, romantic, the surrounding treeless mountains in a massive hug around the valley's visitor. Rocks, heather, sheep – every few metres, winding streams float down a mountain side.

*I am Kerry like my mother before me,
And my mother's mother and her man.
Now I sit on an office stool remembering,
And the memory of them like a fan
Soothes the embers into flame.
I am Kerry and proud of my name.*

*My heart is looped around the rutted hills
That shoulder the stars out of the sky,
And about the wasp-yellow fields
And the strands where the kelp-streamers lie;
Where, soft as lovers' Gaelic, the rain falls,
Sweeping into silver the lacy mountain walls…*

*'Twas thus I lived, skin to skin with the earth,
Elbowed by the hills, drenched by the billows,
Watching the wild geese making black wedges
By Skelligs far west and Annascaul of the willows,
Their voices came on every little wind
Whispering across the half-door of the mind,
For always I am Kerry …*

I am Kerry by Sigerson Clifford.

There are many old stone cottages, long abandoned. They gripped me.

'Stop the car, Tom!' I called, a request I was to make many times during my stay in this beautiful land.

I walked gently in and over and around the rocky landscape that encircled a roofless cottage, wound my way through the stone walls. A hundred years ago this cottage, and the many like it nestled in the valley, would have reverberated with the sounds of husband and wife and possibly a dozen kids going about their daily chores. I could feel these people and the ancients who had inhabited the valley for hundreds of years before them. I could hear their songs, the tapping of their feet as they danced; walked with them as they trudged along the mountain road to take their cattle to town. Families totally reliant on each other.

Tears trickled down my cheeks. Abruptly, I felt grabbed by an unknown force. My tears – were they for peace? Joy? Contentment? Connection? I experienced a one-ness with the land. The unknown force seemed to pull me down, down into the ground, the burial land of my spiritual family, the Brennans. Little did I know that I was to undergo similar experiences, the same pull to the land in the months to come as I travelled round Ireland.

I was in for an epic discovery.

Where are my first born, said the brown land, sighing;
They came out of my womb long, long ago.
They were formed of my dust – why, why are they crying
And the light of their being barely aglow?
I strain my ears for the sound of their laughter
Where are the laws and legend I gave?
Tell me what happened, you who I bore after.
Now only their spirits dwell in the caves.

The First-born
by Jack Davis

This valley, as is the case with many others, especially in the mountainous areas, is deserted now. Privation, famine, emigration all took their toll and the valley was abandoned. And later, much later, the *Celtic Tiger* was born. Only the mountains stand in silent testimony, hold together the songs of the people of old.

I sat back in the car. Tom drove quietly out of the valley. *I must come back here. Until next time.* I wiped a tissue across my face. My *presence* hugged me.

I did not know if Tom realised how deeply this valley experience had affected me. He was born here, grew up in and around these valleys. Dared I say it, dared I presume – he more or less took it for granted? That did not mean he did not appreciate being able to live in the land of his birth, in the mountains that cradled him. For sure, he saw beauty everywhere and I knew he had a deep sense of responsibility to his home, his land. That is why he came back to Kenmare: the profound urge to hold his land, the land of his mother and father, to safeguard it. But did he comprehend the formidable emotions I encountered, the overwhelming occurrence of finally finding my soul?

No one can fully understand the experience of another. In that respect, we need to tread our paths by ourselves. It is a lonely road we must walk. Lonely, yes. But, as I was slowly to prize, tremendously rewarding.

Six

We left Kenmare at about 2 pm and drove directly to Newport, a small village in Co. Tipperary, just over the border of Co. Limerick. It was my first trip north of Killarney.

The day was beautiful, 25 degrees and a cloudless sky. To be sure, there was fainting and wailing in the streets and the farmers tugged at their hair. The plaintive cry, *When will it rain, at all, at all!?* drifted along the 114 kilometres from Killarney to Limerick City. It had not rained in two weeks! I couldn't help but smile as I thought of the months we go without rain in Perth.

Shortly before crossing the border between Limerick and Tipperary, we stopped at Adare, billed as Ireland's prettiest village, although some cynics call it the prettiest 'English' village; such derision, according to my guide book, arises from a perception that the village's manicured perfection is at odds with normal notions of national beauty.

Originally a fief of the Earls of Kildare in 1230, the village owes its present appearance to the Earls of Dunraven, who restored the estate village in the 1830s Tucked in between rows of brightly painted stone buildings, stunningly coloured thatched cottages line Main Street. Some of the roofs were partially split so that the thickness of the thatch could be more easily seen. It is believed that the cottages were the residences of the field labourers who worked the vast tracts of land that made up the Estate.

Adare Village cottage

I suggested to Tom that Adare Manor would be a lovely spot for afternoon tea. Originally a castle, it is now a luxury hotel with accompanying golf course. After driving through magnificent wrought iron gates and weaving through a driveway flanked by acres of luscious green, I gasped at the Manor's magnificence, its location and its architecture: its resplendent Victorian Gothic design. Little did I know that over the ensuing couple of months, I was to be continually confronted by the evidence of the old English stranglehold on the entire country. We strolled around the perimeter of the hotel, then walked towards the main entrance, only to be halted by a porter dressed to the hilt in livery. Without a word, he pointed to a sign near the door: For Residents Only.

'Oh dear! Am awfully sorry!'

As we drove back through the undulating fairways, I remarked, very peevishly, whether this beautiful estate had not passed from one bunch of rich to another – indeed! By the time we had found a quaint cafe and enjoyed a cup of tea and delicious home-baked scones, my crabbiness had abated. Refreshed, we headed off to Newport.

Adare Manor

And in particular, to the townland of Coolrus.

Having visited the village on a previous occasion, Tom drove up a quiet laneway, found the old stone house and parked the car. Various coloured flowering shrubs lined the short path to the front door. A few moments after we had knocked, a woman, of roughly my own age, opened the door. On seeing Tom, her blue eyes opened with surprise, a wide smile took over her face as she greeted him with a hug and asked why he had not rung to tell them of his proposed visit. At the same time, she sent me a quizzical glance.

Tom introduced me: 'Mary, this is Elizabeth.'

'Oh, my,' Mary cried, 'John will be so shocked.'

With that, she ushered us in, poked her head around an old wooden banister, threw back her head and yelled:

'Quick, quick, Son. Run out into the bottom field and tell your father that Fr. Tom is here – and he's got with him your dad's cousin – all the way from Australia!'

While I had learned little of my 'Irish Brennan' heritage during childhood, I often wondered about any Brennan relatives. Did I have any Brennan cousins? If so, where were they?

Gran, my paternal grandmother, and my father's sisters, Aunty Joan and Aunty Benita, my Godmother – both unmarried – were a comforting presence in my younger years. I remember excitedly walking home from school every Tuesday in anticipation of a special after-school treat: iced finger buns which Gran brought with her each weekly visit during which she willingly did odd jobs for my mother. My grandmother was a seamstress, to use her own language, and spent the day darning and ironing and bits and pieces of sewing. Afternoon tea over, she would don her hat and gloves, the only ones I had ever seen her in, and walk down the street to catch the 5 pm tram home.

Over the last 25 years or so, I have learned more of my family tree.

My great-grandfather, Christopher Brennan, was born in Co. Kildare, sometime between November 1843 and November 1844, the son of Michael Brennan, a labourer, and Sarah, nee Pheele (or Fail). My great-grandfather became an apprentice at the Guiness Brewery in Dublin and, when he was about twenty years of age, migrated to New South Wales, where he subsequently worked at Tooth's Kent brewery before becoming a publican in Sydney's inner city.

My great-grandmother was born Mary Anne Carroll, between 2nd and 25th November 1847. Her birthplace was Coolrus, near Cashel in Co. Tipperary. Little is known of her life before she married other than that both of my great-grandparents migrated separately from Ireland and would probably not have known each other prior to their arrival in Australia.

As Axel Clark points out in his book, *Christopher Brennan: A critical biography* (a book that tells the story of their eldest son, my grandfather's brother, a major Australian poet) a 'fundamental fact about the early years of both of Brennan's parents is obvious. The great famine began in Ireland shortly after his [my great-grandfather's] birth and entered one of most terrible phases the year after his mother [my great-grandmother] was born.'

The ancient City of Cashel, near where my great-grandmother was born, had been a stronghold of King Brian Boru. When Boru's descendent, William Smith O'Brien raised a rebellion and brought his Young Irelanders to Cashel in July 1848, he expected to find a city of fire and defiant energy. Instead, he came across a place 'like a city of the dead', all the streets empty, people in despair. Over the following decades, however, as the Irish people recovered their strength and spirit, the famine left many of them with a bitter rebellious determination to *cut the painter* with England. Axel Clark surmises, that in this Irish rebel spirit, 'a new generation of the Brennan family was reared in Sydney.'

One could safely surmise that said horror affected their first born son, who, in years to come, would write in one of his most famous poems, *The Wanderer* –

> *How old is my heart, how old, how old is my heart,*
> *and did I ever go forth with song when the morn was new? ...*
> *The land I came thro' last was dumb with night,*
> *a limbo of defeated glory, a ghost ...*

Christopher Brennan, the brewer, married Mary Carroll at St. Mary's Cathedral, Sydney, on 25th November 1869. On 1st November 1870, their first son was born in Harbour Street, the Haymarket; he was named Christopher John after his father and his mother's father. Mary Brennan subsequently bore many more children, several of whom died in infancy. Four other children survived into adulthood: Agnes Ellen, Teresa Mary, Phillip Benedict and John Felix, my grandfather.

During my childhood, besides my father's mother and his two sisters, the only other Brennan relatives I knew were my grandfather's sisters, Agnes and Theresa, although we all called her 'Aunt Cissy'. I did not know of their connection until later in my life, since my paternal grandparents divorced when my father was still quite young, aged about eight years. I have vague memories of Uncle Phillip, one of my grandfather's brothers, visiting us as well as an even more blurred memory of a single visit by a mysterious man, clothed in a long overcoat. My memory, clouded as it is, tells me that he was my paternal grandfather, John Felix.

Axel Clark, in the Author's note at the beginning of his book on the poet, informs the readers that the first six chapters are taken from a modified version of a Sydney University thesis. It is from these chapters – together with other publications, including an article about the poet in *Eureka: an Irish Australian History Column* published in The Irish Echo by A.P. Quinn, that I source much of what I learned in my adult years about the famous Australian poet.

The young Christopher John Brennan was a sickly child who displayed a promising intelligence and academic aptitude. This combination of poor health and intelligence helped to make him the object of his mother's special attention, whilst isolating him from the robust world of his immediate and extended Irish Catholic family. The young boy received attention and opportunities which were uncommon for one of his social background, and which were not offered to any other members of his family, including my grandfather. Finding that their first-born son showed unusual promise as a student, his parents were ambitious for him, and these ambitions were undoubtedly strengthened by memories of the squalor, privation and disease they had seen in Ireland as children.

In 1880, Christopher became the solitary acolyte at his parish Church and it was assumed by all that he would eventually enter the priesthood. At the age of 14 he secured an academic and boarding scholarship from Cardinal Moran to Sydney's prestigious Jesuit secondary school, St. Ignatius College in Riverview. Life under Jesuit tutelage impacted heavily upon the young boy. He grew into a strong youth and experienced a major intellectual awakening: Jesuit teaching promoted both academic discipline and intellectual freedom. The Classics master, Fr. Patrick Keating, influenced him both morally and intellectually. Captivated by the priest's discipline, grace, sophistication and, above all else, his air of perfection, the young man was marked for a life-long quest for a similar perfection.

As he abandoned the idea of joining the priesthood – a decision that distressed his parents – and with the total support of Cardinal Moran and his Jesuit mentors, he entered the University of Sydney in 1888 where, as a student, he became renowned for his undergraduate pranks and the apparent ease with which he achieved outstanding results whilst neglecting set work and texts. This mistaken description of the young Brennan was removed from the reality: Christopher, in drawing on memories of Jesuit discipline, worked very hard at classical texts of his choice which left him with a general love and intimate understanding of scholarly classical work. He graduated with a Bachelor of Arts in 1891 and the university gold Medal in logic and philosophy. After a brief period at St. Patrick's College in Goulburn, where he wrote his earliest surviving poetry, in 1892 he won the James King of Irrawang Travelling Scholarship and studied at the University of Berlin until 1894.

During his time in Berlin, he became deeply interested in the Symbolist poets, and above all Mallarmé. The Symbolists were not easy to understand. Despite having outwardly abandoned his Catholic heritage, the young man was offered by the Symbolists to 'find the truth where many had sought it.' This truth was not the sort that an ingenious detective might find. It was a religious truth that lay at the heart of the mystery of life. Thus, the young

Christopher was prepared to seek perfection, the ideal he had inherited from his days at Riverview College, through the mundane issues and happenings of daily life, in particular the search for 'perfect' love hidden in the depths of human relationships. This was a search that was to bring him a personal life studded with disappointments, loves won, loves lost, battles with drink, eccentricity, derision, scandal, abandonment and poverty. However, although during his lifetime his poetry was seen as outside the mainstream of Australian poetic development in relation to poets such as Lawson and Patterson, he achieved a posthumous legend as one of Australia's greatest poets, one who helped to create a national literary tradition. This was a search that was to generate the epic poems of *Lillith* and *The Wanderer*, poems that Brennan himself saw as a continuous attempt, together with his other poems, to form what he called 'a concerted poem in many movements.'

While in Germany, he fell in love with Elizabeth Werth, who, together with her mother, followed him back to Sydney. They married and had four children: Christopher, Anna, Rudolph and Elsie. The marriage, tainted by the influence of Elizabeth's mother – who had thought her daughter's husband was going to bring untold riches – was not perfect. Seen as scandalous, his open affair with Violet Léonie Singer – a relationship in which the desperate poet sought the elusive perfection – resulted in his dismissal as Professor at Sydney University in 1922. In the ensuing years, he fell into disgrace, supported financially only by some close friends. In mid-1932, Christopher Brennan died of cancer. Brennan Hall within St. Johns' College at the University of Sydney, is named in his memory.

An article in *The Daily Mirror* on 24th February 1948 declares: *Bohemian Professor whose genius was ignored in his own country* and quotes Shakespeare as saying:

'Heaven doth with us as we with torches do, not light them for themselves'. The author suggests that 'it is a saying exemplified in the lives of all of us, who, even in our most selfish actions, serve purposes not our own; but it is pre-eminently true of those men to whom we apply the title of "genius", whose lives are consumed to produce the blaze of their great works and acts.'

I dwelt with my unpublished screed
Among the untrodden ways
A bard whom there were few to read
And fewer still to praise.

A fungus by a mossy oak
Deep hidden in the grass;
Clear as a star, when turpid smoke
Obscures the optic glass.

Remote I lived, and few could know
If e'er I wrote or how;
But William made his war, and oh!
I'm in the papers now.

Reflections of a Retired Symbolist Poet 1916
Christopher Brennan

Axel Clark closes his monumental book by saying,

Brennan's place in Australian literature is as paradoxical as his character ... with his clotted diction and extreme Victorian poeticism he could not represent a model to be followed by the generations of poets who succeeded him. [However] some of the most important Australian poets of (the twentieth) century – such as R.D. Fitzgerald, A.D. Hope, Judith Wright and James McAuley – have found in his work a point of reference and departure, because he was the first Australian poet to write with (and to be worthy of) the great European philosophical-poetic tradition.

Clark asserts that Christopher J. Brennan undoubtedly stands 'at the head of a remarkably vigorous Australian tradition of intellectual poetry.'

Like many men of his time, my father found it difficult to settle down after World War II. He was a journalist, and had covered and written of the war right up in the front lines.

> *Brennan? He was a war correspondent for the Bulletin, covering the Pacific war in World War II. To describe him properly it is best to quote the united Press correspondent, 'Doc' Quigg, writing from Korea in 1950.*
>
> *"You can say what you want, this war will never really be official until Long John Brennan ambles on to the premises ... When Pacific war correspondents get together to talk over old times, his name leads all the rest ... Here was a man about six and a half feet tall, his height abetted by one of those broad-brimmed Australian soldier's hats ... His rail-lean body, gaunt, ascetic face and saintly, if slightly mangy, beard evoked a nickname ... John was known as the Messiah. He had a habit in invasions and other battles of moseying around a couple of hundred yards ahead of front lines, just so he could be sure of what was going on ... On New Georgia, in the Solomon Islands, he went on an action with a marine raider battalion, and helped bring out wounded. He was scheduled to be decorated by the American army, but some quirk of international protocol prevented it. Again in the Philippines, he went out and got a wounded man under fire. They wanted to give him a medal but could never figure out how to do it."*
>
> Notice in *The Bulletin* on 11th May 1982

Well do I remember the day when we bought a caravan, a trailer-like contraption that opened up into an A-frame two-bed van. We travelled from town to town, our sole income dependent on how many picture frames my father managed to sell. After some time, my older brother and sister, twins, were sent to live in Sydney with Gran so they could attend school; this left just me and a younger brother with our parents. When the time came for another member to join the family, my parents returned to Sydney. Having nowhere to live, we all moved into the small cottage in Naremburn, owned by my grandfather's sister, Aunty Agnes. With the birth of a sister, there were now seven of us.

During cold, wet winter days, the stairs to the attic and the small hallway at the front of the cottage from which they rose became our playground. A favourite game – Lord help us – was 'Mass'. Carl, the older brother, of course was always the priest; my younger brother, John, his altar boy. Carl's twin sister, Margarita, and I were the congregation/choir. Although I was only six years of age, even at that time I thought it most unfair that Carl was always the priest. A feminist in the making?

When we moved into her attic, Aunty Agnes was quite old, possibly in her late 70s, a widow. One day, the young Irish curate from the local parish called at the house to give Aunty Holy Communion. As he made to leave the cottage, I grabbed his hand and kissed it. Mother was horrified! Her words seared into my young brain.

'Elizabeth. NEVER, EVER do that. Those hands hold the Body and Blood of Christ.'

Although, at that time in my life, I did not know how Aunty Agnes was connected to our family, I was aware of the genuine fondness my mother had for her. I don't know how long we stayed in the attic before moving to Balmoral where Nana and Papa – my mother's parents – lived. This was another small house in which some of us slept in a converted veranda whilst my grandparents slept in a caravan in the back yard. My brother, Paul, was born during this time, which necessitated yet another move, this time to my paternal grandmother's house. Gran and the two aunts, Joan and Benita, found a small flat elsewhere and gave the old Brennan house to us. Of great fascination to me was a brass plate at the front door with the word 'Coolrus' boldly emblazoned upon it. I had never seen a house that had its own name!

While not able to remember specific conversations, in later years I came to understand that Coolrus was originally owned by my great-grandmother, Mary Anne Brennan (nee Carroll) who bequeathed it to her daughter, Agnes, who in turn passed it on to her sister-in-law Josephine, my grandmother. Coolrus was the name of the townland in Co. Tipperary in Ireland in which she was born.

Years passed, yet more brothers and sisters joined the fold. And I continued to wonder about my Brennan heritage. Although immersed in an Irish theology at school, in the Parish and at home, as I entered my adolescent years, I still did not know my roots were in Ireland.

On the first day of high school, Sister Martina, my Latin teacher, when marking the role, looked over the class when she called my name.

'Are you a relation to Christopher Brennan?' she sternly quizzed.

I looked at her, puzzled, dumbstruck. I had not heard of this man before. I confronted my mother on my return home. She informed me that my Aunt Cissy used to be a nun, in the same Mercy Order from which Sister Martina came, the Order which ran the school. Aunt Cissy, my mother continued, had left the convent, a disgrace in those times. It was a closely-guarded family secret; only one of many I was to learn only in my later years. My mother could not tell me of this person Christopher Brennan. My father had never mentioned his name before. Actually, he never spoke to me, at all! Other than when reprimanding me for yet another of my faults. It was not until well into my adult years that I understood more about my father and where he came from: a boy who grew up without a father, a man who did not know what 'fathering' entailed.

Ah! what bliss to have the knowledge and understanding of an adult. To know – and understand – more clearly the lack of input in my younger years into the Brennan side of my family. Although I knew, during the days of my youth, that my paternal grandparents were not together, I did not appreciate the extent of the hardship this caused my grandmother. She worked long hours as a seamstress to support her young family, my father and his two younger sisters, and was, quite possibly, very bitter towards the Brennans, and such bitterness passed on to her children. In later years, I had opportunities to talk with my father's sisters and, although coloured by their own perceptions, they filled me in on some of the Brennan history.

It was Papa Gotsch – my maternal grandfather – who introduced me, in my early 20s, to Christopher Brennan, the poet. The story I gleaned was that, in his younger bohemian years, Papa – a struggling German musician in post-World War I Sydney – was very impressed by Christopher Brennan, an icon in Sydney's intellectual circles of the time. Christopher Brennan, he told me, was my great-uncle, my grandfather's brother. Papa gave me my first collection of Christopher Brennan's poetry.

Time moved on. I moved on.

After moving to Western Australia in 1975, I was determined to prove that I could do other things than successfully give birth. When my fifth child was two years old, I enrolled in night school to study for the Mature Age Matriculation. When my first assignment in English Literature was returned to me, the tutor paid me – in what I deemed a surprised voice – a compliment on its quality. I puffed out my dried up breasts, raised my chin, stared down my nose:

'Christopher Brennan was my great-uncle!'

'Ah, that explains it!' he replied.

Little did he know I was none the wiser.

And I continued to wonder about my Brennan heritage.

In the mid 90s, John Stephenson published a book, *The Optimist*. I read a review of the book, a work of fiction, based on the years Christopher Brennan spent in Goulburn when he was a young man. I was hooked. I wrote to the author care of his publisher in Sydney, told him who I was – a Brennan! John rang me. During our telephone call, he spoke of a recent conversation he had had with the grandson of the poet, another Christopher Brennan, who lived in Kindee, mid-coast New South Wales. I procured his telephone number from Telstra and dialled. A deep voice answered.

'Hello. Uh, uh,' I stammered. 'My name is Elizabeth Brennan and I believe we are related.'

He was as gob-smacked as I was. Not only did I learn that, indeed, I have Brennan cousins, I discovered that one lived here in the West! And only a few suburbs away!! Again, I tentatively picked up the phone.

During my next visit to the East Coast, I met John Stephenson for lunch at a pub in Newtown and we were joined by Axel Clarke who had written the critical biography of Brennan. They took me on a 'Brennan tour of Sydney'; showed houses he had lived in, pubs his father, my great grandfather, owned and others the poet had frequented. At the end of the day, Axel presented me with a signed copy of his book.

I stayed overnight with my mother at Forster, from which I proceeded to Kindee and met my cousin. As I looked deep into his smiling, familiar face, I experienced a deep sense of peaceful concretization, a certainty that I was on the way to discovering who I was. Chris's and his wife Pat's home nestled in gently rolling, deep green hillocks upon which grazed a few contented cows. Utter bliss. We dined leisurely and spoke as if we had always known each other. Childless, he told me that he and his sister, the mother of the cousins in Perth, were the only remaining direct descendants of the poet – together with the West Australian cousins.

On my arrival home in the West, I assiduously read and re-read Axel's biography and came to understand and appreciate the genius of Christopher Brennan and came also to understand a little more about myself. A Scorpio like the poet, I contentedly placed myself as a 'romantic' in the literary sense. A constant theme that wove through his poetry was a belief that perfection and self-actualisation, a culmination of pure desire, was to be found in human love. Together with this premise was an acknowledgement of the paradox experienced in this quest. On a search on the internet, I came across a poem by Francis Duggan, posted on PoemHunter.com that, in part, said:

> *The great Sydney poet Christopher John Brennan was in a class of his own*
> *Yet lesser lights than him seem far better known...'*

Nothing unusual about this in the history of Australian literature.

The more I read, the more I came to 'know' this brother of my grandfather and finally connected to my roots: I am a Brennan, I am Irish. After almost half a century, I gleaned a sense of who I might be. Wow!

From there on, I whole-heartedly endeavoured to discover family connections in Ireland. With the help of an Irish friend who went 'home' for a prolonged visit, I made contact with John Joe. His great grandfather and Mary Ann Carroll, my great grandmother, were siblings.

A year after my discovery of the continued occupation of the Carrolls at Coolrus, on his next visit 'home', Tom drove to Tipperary and met John Joe and Mary.

Unfortunately, to date, all my endeavours to discover any of my Brennans in Ireland have borne no fruit. Since Brennan is amongst the top most common names in Ireland this is somewhat understandable. But I soldier on.

John Joe trod through the front door, a smile cemented across his weathered face. 'Welcome, cousin! We've waited a long time!'

Tears coursed down my cheeks, whiskey was poured and the long evening began. Conversation, whiskey, laughter, whiskey, more talk, whiskey – went on and on. I brought out the few photos I had with me just for this occasion, in particular one of me and my three daughters at my mother's wake.

'And don't you look as young as them?' Mary remarked. 'It could be a photo of four sisters sure! Who would believe it?'

Neighbours, alerted to the special occasion, filed in and introductions were made: 'Meet my cousin from Australia! And isn't she lovely! Mother of God, lovely she is!' My Irish eyes smiled and smiled – amid the tears.

Of course, as I had come to know, no Irish visit is complete without a *walk up the road*. John Joe escorted Tom and me, pointing out the different neighbours' houses. All my childhood fantasies came to life! The farms were so different from Australian farms, not that I am an expert on Australian farms. For one thing, the houses were built right on the road – no long driveway to the house – and, of course, from my stand point, so small. The country roads have evolved from cow tracks from one farm to another, according to John Joe's continuous monologue. Original tracks went from one house to another, the cabins and cottages built long before the roads. A *walk up the road* inevitably involves a visit to the Church – and the adjacent graveyard.

On our return, we eagerly dug into the meal Mary had prepared.

To be sure, I had to keep reminding myself that I was sitting in the kitchen of the house in which my great-grandmother had been born. At one point in the evening, John Joe remarked that he did not know what would happen to the farm – his children were not interested in staying in Tipperary. I drew my lips tight; wanted to scream out, 'Hey, I'll take it on. I'm family!'

I had attempted many times to ring John Joe to inform him of our visit but he did not answer and there was no answering machine. Hence, because they were not expecting us, we took our leave after assured promises of meeting again.

Oh yes! I would be back. The newly-connected Carroll blood flowed warmly through my Brennan veins.

John Joe and Mary Carroll and myself in front of the house in which my great-grandmother was born –
Coolrus in Co. Tipperary

As we drove towards Tipperary City, I could not help but remember the poem Mary Carrol's son wrote so many years after her migration to Australia, a poem that, to me, sums up his life-long quest to find self-actualisation in human love; a poem that also symbolized my quest to connect to my roots.

If questioning could make us wise
no eyes would ever gaze in eyes;
if all our tale were told in speech
no mouths would wander each to each.

Were spirits free from mortal mesh
And love not bound in hearts of flesh
no aching breasts would yearn to meet
and find their ecstasy complete.

For who is there that live and knows
the secret powers by which he grows?
Were knowledge all, what were our need
to thrill and faint and sweetly bleed?

Then seek not, sweet, the If and Why
I love you now until I die
For I must love because I live
And life in me is what you give.

                                          Christopher Brennan

Ah, yes, and ain't I open to what this country can give? Ain't I open to the reality that the life in me will be what this country bestows on a searching, forlorn soul?'

Seven

We had intended to tour the Lower Shannon around the City of Limerick and up the west coast. However, after our visit with John Joe, the fine weather had broken and Tom suggested it was not a good time to see the west. I silently stared through the car window, wondered at the softly falling rain as it mirrored my heart. I shook myself from the momentary despair, confident I would be back at Coolrus soon.

Tom drove south east towards Tipperary city and stopped at a small village called Pallas Green. After enquiries from a pub, we found a B&B, booked in and returned to the pub for a pint.

After a good sleep and hearty Irish breakfast, the next day we continued south east through Tipperary City towards Cashel and stopped off to view Athassel Priory. This ruined Augustinian monastery is situated on the west bank of the River Suir. I was fascinated to learn that it was established in 1192 and is believed to have been the largest medieval priory until it was burned down in 1447 by Cromwell. The tomb of William de Burgh, the founder of the priory, lies in the ruined church.

Throughout all my travels, I never got over the number of ruined castles and churches throughout Ireland. They seem to just pop up, over many a bend or rise in the road. Is it the same in Europe or England? Most of the damage was perpetrated by Oliver Cromwell and his armies. Was there equal religious suppression on the Continent? Is its landscape furrowed by ruins that silently decry their deliberate desecration?

Another thing I noticed, typically Irish. Dare I say that, a mere visitor? I could not see any speed signs on the roads. A lot of notices warning four demerit points for speeding, but no way of knowing what the speed limit was! Tom told me that speed is a big problem in Ireland – but how do you know what the speed limit was? Ah, to be sure, everyone knows it is 60 kph – why bother with signs?

In Cashel, I ambled along the almost deserted street back to the car, relishing the warmth of the thick bowl of soup we had enjoyed at a small pub. I passed a shoe shop. I tell you, I had never seen such beautiful shoes. A woman with a very deep passion for shoes – which some dare to describe as a fetish! – I was transfixed by the window display. Conscious of my all-too casual attire, I entered and asked where the shoes were from. Spain, most of them. Fancy finding such a shop in Cashel! Why don't we have such splendour available in Perth! Or do we, and I don't know about such luxury and extravagance? Do I not shop in the right stores?

The weather still wet, we decided to leave a visit to the famous Cashel Rock, where Patrick baptised the King of Munster, until a later time and drove north towards Thurles where we visited the Holy Cross Abbey. Founded in 1168 by the King of Munster for the Benedictines, it was transferred in about 1182 to the Cistercians who built much of its present structure. The Abbey is purported to house a particle of the True Cross; hence its name. After standing roofless for 200 years, it was fully restored as part of European Architectural Heritage in 1969. Now used as a parish church, I learned it is one of the finest examples of late Gothic architecture in Ireland.

From Thurles, we went north to Roscrea and drove to St. Joseph's Abbey, one of the few practising Cistercian Abbeys remaining, as they have rooms for guests. Unfortunately, they were booked out – disappointing as it would have been interesting to 'be with the monks' for a short time. We headed for town and booked into a hotel. During a meal, I read some of the history of the town. Owing to the numerous remains of various religious houses, Roscrea is known as a Monastic Town, dominated by St. Cronin's Monastery and Roscrea Castle. Roscrea is strategically located in a gap between the Slieve Bloom and Devil's Bit mountains, so called because, according to legend, the devil took a bite out of the mountain. He supposedly broke some teeth which then formed the Rock of Cashel. Roscrea was on one of the great roads of early historic Ireland, the Slighe Dála (meaning parliament way) which stretched from Tara in the east to the city and port of Limerick in the west. As I anticipated a fabulous tour of the famous Roscrea Castle on the morrow, coupled with a realisation that I would need to take copious notes for my three grandsons in Perth – 'Wow! You went to a *real* castle, Granma?' – I snuggled deep beneath the doona, recalled, with a wry smile, the information I had read of St. Cronin's. Originally a Catholic place of worship, it now belongs to the Church of Ireland.

As I drifted off to sleep, a picture of a young girl surfaced. A young girl who, in her formative years, was only aware of two types of people: Catholics and Publics. A young girl who, during the school lunch break, stood on tip toe to lean over the wooden fence in order to peer at the equally young girls in the school playground on the other side of the road: *There go the Publics! There go the Catholics!* we taunted each other in turn. And here, in Roscrea in the centre of Ireland, I was reading about the Catholics and the Protestants! How many wars have been fought – are still being fought – because of religious intolerance and prejudice? Will we – human beings – ever really accept that people can just 'be'?

At breakfast the next day, yet again with eyes glued to a brochure full of Roscrea's history, I learned that Roscrea is the birthplace of Daisy Bates, a woman of whom all I knew was that she spent 35 years of her life in the deserts of Australia, living with, and studying and compiling 'voluminous' reports on Aboriginal people. Whilst in my youth she had been lauded as a courageous woman who showed great love and concern for the Indigenous peoples of Australia, she was also controversial in that she asserted that 'they ate their babies.' Little did I know, whilst enjoying my Irish breakfast, that a few short months later on Saturday January 1, 2005, Professor Bob Reece from Murdoch University would give a talk at Manning Clarke House in Canberra titled 'You would have loved her for her lore'. He later published a book, *Grand Dame of the Desert*, reviewed in *The West Australian*, in which he painted her as a bigamist and a liar.

Born as Margaret Dwyer in Roscrea in 1859, she migrated to Australia when she was 23 after a presumable sexual scandal whilst employed as a governess in Dublin, which resulted in the young man of the house committing suicide. By the time she arrived in Australia, she had changed her name to Daisy May O'Dwyer, setting a pattern for the rest of her life of continuous re-invention of her history. It is recorded that, in 1884, she married 'Breaker' Morant, who was infamously executed for war crimes committed during the Second Boer War. Shortly after the marriage, she left him because he had not paid for the wedding. There is no record of a divorce. In 1885, Daisy married John (Jack) Bates, who, like Morant, was a breaker of wild horses, a bushman and a drover. The bigamous nature of this marriage was kept a secret during Daisy Bates' lifetime.

I did enjoy my breakfast!

Also of interest, I learned the meaning of the word Roscrea: Crea means wood and Ros, a woman's name. The original Ros, a Gaelic chieftain's wife, owned all the surrounding forest. This was not an unusual circumstance: women played an active part in everyday affairs. They had legal rights which included rights to own and inherit property. I also learned, though with not quite an equal degree of envy, that women often accompanied their husbands into battle and, in some cases, even joined in the fighting. *Cúchulainn* is an Irish mythological hero who was trained as a warrior by two women, Skatha and Aife. This is an indication of the high place women were held in ancient, pre-Christian Ireland unlike their Roman counterparts. W.B. Yeats used the hero as a national symbol in much of his poetry as seen in his cycle of Cúchulainn. The first poem, *The Death Of Cúchulainn*, was published in 1882; the last in the cycle, *Cúchulainn Comforted*, published in 1939.

Ah, is it any wonder, at all at all, that my soul, from its youthful years, yearned for this land that honoured its women – even though the human form, in which this yearning, pre-pubescent feminist soul was cradled, was not aware of this sacred land's ancient history! Indeed, did not this craving soul resent that she could not play the role of priest in her games with her brothers! Alas, did she learn too late of her Irish fore-mothers' status?

The husband-to-be shall pay a bride-price of land, cattle, horses, gold or silver to the father of the bride.
Husband and wife retain individual rights to all the land, flocks and household goods each brings to the marriage.

The husband who, through listlessness, does not go to his wife in her bed, must pay a fine.

If a pregnant woman craves a morsel of food and her husband withholds it through stinginess or neglect, he must pay a fine.

Brehon Laws.

Prior to a visit to the castle, we returned to St. Joseph's Abbey where I was fortunate to meet a real live, practising Cistercian monk, in habit and all. The Cistercians, I was gravely informed, are an off-shoot of the Benedictines. Their founder, St. Canice, believed that the Benedictines had strayed from the path laid down by their revered founder and thus Canice formed his own Order. Cistercians evidently do not speak unnecessarily: prayer and work is of utmost importance.

I bowed my head reverently, prayed that my work in exploring the castle would be rewarded.

The castle was built by the Normans in 1213 – originally an earthwork and timber structure – as a defense fort. In recent times, the moat that surrounded the castle has been diverted and is now a stream that winds its way through the narrow streets of the old monastic town. We crossed the still-standing drawbridge that spanned the moat. I spied a hole in the castle wall high above the bridge. In times past, hot oil was poured upon any un-welcomed visitors. If this did not deter the intruders, arrows were shot from another hole. Yet again, any such determined visitors were eventually driven out by sharp arrow-like shafts of iron which protruded from the gate.

Roscrea Castle

Thankfully without being doused with hot oil, we entered the castle and began to climb a steep winding staircase, the steps of which were of an uneven height and width; a staircase that, unusually, wound clockwise. Such configuration was intended to make it very difficult for would-be assassins to draw their swords from a left-handed scabbard. Despite these menacing obstacles, we accomplished the climb and entered a massive hall where the castle inhabitants congregated for meals. I stood in awe in front of the largest fireplace imaginable above which was a tiny room with a window that looked out into the hall. During the years of the great plague and with the strong belief that wandering minstrels brought disease, the owners assigned this place for them to perform and, therefore, the castle residents could dance and be amused without fear. To further ensure their safety, a wardroom and toilet was situated off the hall. Clothes were hung along the walls of the room with the absolute assurance that the odour of urine and faeces would kill any lingering disease. The toilet bowl was huge, and, naturally, the pipe that led from it was spiral in shape, thus guaranteeing that no intruder could fire an arrow upwards whilst someone was so enthroned. I stood in utter admiration of the ancient people's ingenuity.

Instead of glass in the windows, sheep and cow stomachs were dried and stretched till they became transparent. Of course, there was no need for bedrooms or dormitories. The soldiers slept sitting upright against the stone walls in full armour in readiness for any surprise attack.

In fear and horror, I bent to peer into the prison-dungeon. The only entrance was a small hole in which people were thrown into the deep abyss. I trembled at the realisation, because of the closeness of the moat, of the probable degree of the dungeon's damp and icy environment.

All but a small section of the walls of the castle still stand; the town evolved and grew around it, dwellings built right up to the old stone walls.

Inside Roscrea Castle

In the 18th century, a town house was built in the grounds of the castle by the Butler family. The family's ancestor, a butler to the English king, in return for his competence and loyalty, was granted the castle and allowed to retain the name Butler. Damer House, as it was called, has been converted into a museum. In a back room, I gazed upon an incredible collection of modern art and sculpture, all created from bogwood, the designer of which is a local. He fashions the pieces for his own gratification and donates them to the museum. He refuses payment for any of his work.

From Roscrea, we headed east and then south to a place called Donaghmore, still in Co. Tipperary, to visit a museum – an old famine workhouse.

In a phone call to Australia, I had been asked by my daughter, Ally, if there was much evidence of the Great Famine in Ireland. To be sure, to be sure, it was all around, wherever we went. Huge, massive castles and manor houses, vast tracts of land walled in by three metre high thick stone walls, built to keep the people – the peasants – out.

I learned that Central Ireland in particular suffered most by the famine years and prior to that, the centuries of suffering in the Penal years when people were not allowed to practise their Catholic faith. This is not to say, of course, that the people did not suffer in other parts of Ireland. In Kenmare, there are ruins of a workhouse in which thousands of people suffered. In Counties Laios, Kilkenny and Tipperary, many high walls follow the roads. Evidently, Central Ireland is the most prosperous farming land and the English owned all the land in the past.

The wind and rain whips round me. Is this summer in Ireland? I stop, as stop I must, just out of Tipperary City. Perched along the slopes of a small hill is an old Famine Memorial Graveyard. I tread softly up the slope, which is dotted with images depicting the Stations of the Cross; am suddenly unable to move further. My heart aches, tears flow. I succumb to the tears; move on. Although, as a sign depicts, the site is well looked after by a group of people in the City, it appears desolate, lonely. Are the dead alone?

Not alone is the learned history of my great-grandmother and great-grandmothers before her. Of men and women whose right to their land, their customs, their religion, was taken from them. Not alone is the story of a mother and father who, despite their miraculous survival of the Great Famine, during which many of their family members perished, had nothing to offer their youngest child but their ardent prayers. A mother and father, born and buried up the road in Co. Tipperary, forced to farewell a young girl when there was nothing for her but to travel to the other side of the world. A young girl who, despite her tears and fears, held her head high in a strange land. A young girl who met and married a man from Co. Kildare. A young girl, whose great-granddaughter plies her way through the Stations on a windy hill in Tipperary.

At Donaghmore, a few kilometres from Tipperary City, rising out of a bleak stretch of land, is a workhouse museum. The reality of what people suffered stuns me. Only in desperation did they go to the workhouse. Families were split up – husbands from wives, parents from children. There were extended stone 'beds' along the floor, on which they slept; the only heat available was from their own emaciated bodies. The workhouse is huge: hundreds of people worked there for a small portion of food. When they died, their bodies were thrown into mass graves.

Donaghmore Workhouse

Some years prior to my trip, I had read *The Great Hunger* by Cecil Woodham Smith, first published in 1962 and considered by many as the most accurate summation of the causes and effects of the Great Famine in Ireland during the years 1845-1849. From my reading, I reached a deeper understanding of the word 'famine' and what it entails. A famine is not just a shortage of food brought about by drought, flood, or in the case of the Irish Famine, a blight that affected the potato. In simple terms, such shortage of food and a resultant famine is inflamed by the aggressive demands of the economic market.

The famine was a watershed in the history of Ireland. Its effects permanently changed the island's demographic, political and cultural landscape. For both the native Irish and those in the resulting diaspora, the famine entered folk memory and became a rallying point for various nationalist movements. Many modern historians regard it as a dividing line in the Irish historical narrative, referring to the preceding period of Irish history as 'pre-famine'.

In the forty years that followed the Act of Union, in which Ireland officially became part of the United Kingdom, successive British governments grappled with the problems of governing a country which had, as Benjamin Disraeli put it in 1844, a "starving population, an absentee aristocracy, and an alien Church, and in addition the weakest executive in the world." The result of 114 commissions and 61 special committees conducted between 1801 and 1845, predicted that Ireland was on the verge of starvation; her population was rapidly increasing; three-quarters of her labourers were unemployed; housing conditions were appalling and the standard of living unbelievably low.

The remaining notorious Penal Laws, which were inaugurated around 1607 – and rigorously enforced by Oliver Cromwell – were finally repealed about 50 years before the famine. The Laws were put in place in an endeavour to force Roman Catholics and dissenting Protestant Churches, such as the Presbyterians, to convert to the reformed Christian Church of England. The Laws prohibited Irish Catholics and dissenters from owning or leasing land; from voting; from holding political office; from living in a corporate town or within eight kilometres of a corporate town; from obtaining education and from entering a profession and from doing many other things that were necessary in order to succeed and prosper in life. Although the final Laws had been revoked, the economic recovery was slow because the landlord families still kept their land. This exacerbated the effects of the Potato Famine

Catholics made up 80% of the population, the bulk of whom still lived in conditions of poverty and insecurity. At the top of the social pyramid was the 'ascendancy class', the English and Anglo-Irish families who owned most of the land and who had more or less limitless power over their tenants. During the 18th century, a new system for managing the landlord's property was introduced in the form of the 'middleman system'. Rent collection was left in the hands of the landlords' agents, or middlemen. The revenue was sent to England, collected from impoverished tenants who were paid minimal wages to raise crops and livestock for export. This assured the (usually Protestant) landlord of a regular income, and relieved them of any responsibility; the tenants however were then subject to exploitation through these middlemen.

According to Cecil Woodham-Smith, the ability of the middlemen was measured by the amount of money they could contrive to extract and send to the absentee landlords, with some visiting their property once or twice in a lifetime, if ever. As a result of the power in which the absentee landlords, through their middlemen, used without remorse, the people of Ireland lived in dread of them and, says Woodham-Smith, 'industry and enterprise were extinguished and a peasantry created which was one of the most destitute in Europe'. An 1841 census showed a population of just over eight million. Two-thirds of those depended on agriculture for their survival, but they rarely received a working wage. They had to work for their landlords in return for the small patch of land they needed in order to grow enough food for their families.

The potato was introduced to Ireland as a garden crop for the gentry. By the late 17th century, it had become widespread as a supplementary rather than a principal food, as the main diet still revolved around butter, mill and grain products. By 1815, the potato had become a base food for the poor all year round.

The Celtic grazing lands of Ireland had been used to pasture cows for centuries. When the British colonised the Irish, they transformed much of the countryside into an extended grazing land to raise cattle for a hungry consumer market at home. The British taste for beef had a devastating impact on the impoverished and disenfranchised people of Ireland. Pushed off the best pasture land and forced to farm smaller plots of marginal land, the Irish turned to the potato, a crop that could be grown abundantly in a less favourable soil. For the labourer, the potato wage essentially shaped the expanding agrarian economy.

In 1844, Irish newspapers carried reports concerning a disease which for two years had attacked the potato crops in America. It is suggested that ships from Baltimore, Philadelphia or New York could have brought diseased potatoes to European ports. On 13 September, 1845 the *Gardeners' Chronicle* made a dramatic announcement: 'We stop the Press with very great regret to announce that the potato Murrain has unequivocally declared itself in Ireland'. By November 19, 1845 it was ascertained by the Mansion House Committee in Dublin that 'considerably more than one-third of the entire of the potato crop ... has been already destroyed.'

In 1846, three quarters of the harvest was lost to blight. Seed potatoes were scarce in 1847 – little had been sown. As a result, in 1848 yields would be only two thirds of normal. As over 3 million Irish people totally depended on potatoes for food, hunger and destitution were inevitable.

Whilst various suggestions were put forward to deal with 'the Irish problem', the principal stand the British Parliament took was to preserve, at all costs, the free market.

In 1845, the Prime Minister Sir Robert Peel secretly purchased £100,000 worth of maize and cornmeal from America. The government hoped that it would not 'stifle private enterprise' and that its actions would not act as a disincentive to local relief efforts. Due to weather difficulties, the first shipment did not arrive in Ireland until the beginning of February, 1846. The maize, when it arrived, had not been ground and was inedible, which caused severe bowel complaints.

Various attempts were undertaken to introduce public works projects; these endeavours, however, were strictly ordered by Sir Charles Trevelyan, the Administrator of Government Relief , who believed that 'the judgement of God sent the calamity to teach the Irish a lesson'. As a result, the projects proved impossible to administer. Peel's successor, Lord John Russell, persuaded by the laissez-faire belief that the market would provide the food needed whilst at the same time ignoring the massive food exports to England, halted government food and relief works. Private initiatives such as The Central Relief Committee of the Society of Friends (Quakers) attempted to fill the gap caused by the end of government relief. Eventually the government reinstated the relief works, although bureaucracy slowed the release of food supplies.

A clause of the Poor Law prohibited anyone who held at least quarter of an acre from receiving rent. Thus, a farmer, having sold all his produce to pay rent, duties, rates and taxes, reduced, like thousands of others, to apply for public relief, would not get it until he had first delivered up all his land to the landlord. In 1849, approximately 90,000 people were evicted from their land. Landlords were responsible for paying rates of every tenant who paid less than £4 in yearly rent. It was yet another reason to evict poor tenants from their small plots so the landlord could rent out larger plots which reduced their debts.

It is nigh impossible to be sure how many people were evicted during the years of the Famine and its immediate aftermath. It was only in 1849 that the police began to keep a count, and whilst a total of almost 250,000 persons has been officially recorded as being evicted between 1849 and 1854, this number is considered by many to be a gross underestimate and if the sums were to include the number pressured into 'voluntary surrenders', the figure would almost certainly exceed half a million persons. Helen Litton – author of *The Irish Famine: An Illustrated History*, among other books on the famine – suggests that there was 'precious little voluntary' in these surrenders; in many cases, tenants were persuaded to accept a small sum of money to leave their homes, 'cheated into believing the workhouse would take them in'. By 1854, between one and a half and two million Irish left their country due to evictions, starvation and harsh living conditions. Most migrated to the United States of America.

When Ireland experienced a famine in 1782-1783, ports were closed to keep Irish-grown food in Ireland to feed the Irish. Local food prices promptly dropped. The people did not starve, did not die of disease, were not evicted from their homes and sent *walking up the road* whilst their cabins were torn down. The people did not have to trip over corpses during their travels, did not have to leave their kin to die and rot in the muddy ditches. Joseph Crosfield, a Quaker, is said to have witnessed in the Potato Famine a: *heart-rending scene (of) poor wretches in the last stages of famine imploring to be received into the workhouse ... Some of the children were worn to skeletons, their features sharpened with hunger and their limbs wasted almost to the bone.*

Between 1845 and 1849, Ireland remained a net exporter of food to Britain throughout most of the five year famine. Several writers single out the decision of the government to permit the continued export of food from Ireland as a flag of the policy-makers' attitudes; there was ample food in Ireland while all the Irish-bred cattle was shipped off to England. Although I did not see it, written on a mural on the Ballymurphy Road in Belfast is: *An Gorta Mór, Britain's genocide by starvation, Ireland's holocaust.*

There were both religious and non-religious organisations which came to the assistance of famine victims from all parts of the globe. Unfortunately, many of the religious groups' influence for good was marred by a wide-spread system of proselytism, and resultant seeds of bitterness can still be found today.

Weary men, what reap ye? Golden corn for the stranger.
What sow ye? Human corpses that wait for the avenger
Fainting forms, Hunger ... stricken, what see you in the offing
Stately ships to bear our food away, amid the stranger's scoffing.
There's a proud array of soldiers ... what do they round your door?
They guard our master's granaries from the thin hands of the poor.
Pale mothers, wherefore weeping? Would to God that we were dead ...
Our children swoon before us, and we cannot give them bread.

The Famine Year
Jane Francesca Elgee 'Speranza'
carried in *The Nation*

On another occasion, whilst travelling through Co. Roscommon, we visited Stokestown Park House, which was originally built in the 1730's for Thomas Mahon, MP, and stayed in the family till 1979 when it was restored. In 1847, Major Denis Mahon forced two-thirds of the starving peasantry off his land, a total of over 3,000 people. And this was done whilst he and his family were still able to dine on lobster soup.

I slowly walked back to the car, my fingers entwined with those of the *presence*. Everything was still, quiet. No other cars on the road. Silence. I looked back to the way we came; in memory trod back up the slopes of the Famine Memorial Graveyard just outside of Tipperary City. Remembered ....

At each Station, a plaque calls visitors to a particular plight of the people crushed by imperialism, poverty and disenfranchisement. At the Ninth Station – Jesus falls the Third Time – I am urged to commend to God those buried whose names are unknown. How many times must Jesus – must I – must all the Great Mother's people – fall?

Eight

According to my well-thumbed guide book, Kilkenny is Ireland's 'loveliest inland city.' From what I saw, I heartily concur. I *love* Kilkenny.

In 1172, the Norman Knight, Richard de Clare, known as Strongbow, built a wooden tower on a rocky height overlooking the River Nore. This strategic location was, until then, the stronghold of the *Mac Gilla Pátric*, the ancient kings of Ossory. Strongbow ensured his succession to the lordship of Leinster through his marriage to *Aoife*, the daughter and heiress of *Diarmuid Mac Marchadha*, King of Leinster.

Kilkenny continued its rise to prominence and eventually became the medieval capital of Ireland. James Butler, the 3rd Earl of Ormonde – from the same Anglo-Norman family from Roscrea – bought Kilkenny Castle in 1391, thus installing himself as undisputed ruler of the area. The family held sway over the city for 500 years.

We arrived late in the afternoon, booked into a B&B, and headed in to town. The medieval grandeur of many of its restored buildings in a rich variety of dark reds and browns, fronted by arcades once typical of Kilkenny's main streets mesmerised me. Between the two parallel main streets, St. Kieran's Street and High Street, we walked through tiny, narrow alleyways, known locally as 'slips', one of them called the Butter Slip after the butter stalls that once lined the small market place. I could only presume these constricted walkways were called 'slips' because that is what happened – they just 'slipped' in over time. As I walked slowly through the 'slips' I was filled with strong, multiple conflicting emotions: a sense of eeriness and mystical wonderment as if I had landed on a distant planet.

Tom and I in a Butter Slip

We soon worked up an appetite and had no problem locating a cosy pub. Kilkenny is renowned, evidently, by pub lovers: a brewery city for hundreds of years, there are close to 800 official pubs, not counting the popular private drinking clubs! Smethwick's, a popular beer, has been brewed in Kilkenny since 1710.

'Aye, a bit like your own!' Tom said with a grin, referring to my own brewery in a backyard shed at home.

When I first started to brew beer, I did it in the presbytery where Tom lived: he had more storage room than I had at the time. The keg was in the laundry and the sound of the bubbling brew was often quite audible when people came for appointments, either with him or me, as they walked into the hallway at the front of the house.

'A great pot of soup cooking,' was our standard reply to the raised eyebrows. The brew became well known amongst friends as *Liz's Presbyterian Brew*. In later years, after my son-in-law was ordained an Anglican priest, his bishop remarked one day during a meal,

'Ah, Stuart, me boy! You've got the best mother-in-law anyone could wish for!'

Ah, to be sure! And wasn't my great-grandfather a brewer at Guinness' Brewery in Dublin and then, after migrating to Australia, in Circular Quay in Sydney?

An effigy of a witch sits in the window frame of the historic Kyteler's coaching inn, a reminder of the story of a former resident, Dame Alice Kyteler. In 1324, Alice and her maid were pronounced guilty of witchcraft after four of Alice's husbands had died in strange circumstances. When her fourth husband, John le Poer, became sick in 1324, he expressed the suspicion that he was being poisoned. After his death, his children and other family members of her previous husbands, banded together and accused Alice of using poison and sorcery against all her four husbands. The case was brought before the then Bishop of Ossory, Richard de Ledrede, in 1324. Although originally pardoned, Alice was later re-charged a second time after one of her servants, Petronella de Meath, was tortured and confessed to witchcraft and implicated Alice. Dame Alice managed to escape, leaving her maid to burn at the stake.

We walked in to a pub that seemed inviting, the Marble City Bar, and dined on a sumptuous meal of mussels and salmon and, would you believe, couscous! In most of the pubs, the last meal order is taken between 8pm and 9pm. At around about 8.30pm, a small band took its place and the *cráic* began. Sublime! I sat close to the band, enthralled and rapt as usual by the music. Again, as usual, my right hand beat upon my right thigh in time with the guy who played the bodhrán.

The bodhrán is the heartbeat of Irish music. This ancient frame-drum is traditionally made with a wooden body and a stretched goatskin head, and is played with a double-headed stick called a *cipín*, *tipper*, or *beater*. There are at least two cross bows at the back so that the player can hold the drum in one hand and then use the fingers of that hand to beat slightly on the back of the drum. The modern Irish word *bodhrán* is pronounced *bow-rawn*, like *Cow brawn*, with a slight emphasis on the first syllable.

A Bodhrán

During a break, the leader of the band came up to me and said, 'Ah, I see you evidently play the bodhrán!'

I grinned, shook my right hand – neither assenting nor disagreeing with his assumption! We finally left, just after midnight, and as I walked past the band, he waved and said,

'And bring your bodhrán next time, won't ye?' Did I feel ten feet tall!

The following day we visited Kilkenny Castle. Set in a commanding position overlooking the River Nore, this Norman fortress is one of Ireland's most famous castles. Built in the 1190s, by Stronghold's son-in-law, William Marshal, Earl of Pembroke, as mentioned it was bought by the Butler family and occupied by them right up until 1935. With a devastating World War, the final achievement of the Republic of Ireland and tremors all around

Europe, together with the unsustainable cost of maintaining the castle, the Butler family decided the time had come to leave Ireland.

The castle was abandoned and most of the furnishings were auctioned. Many of the local people bought them and when the caste was donated to the nation in 1967, a lot of the previously auctioned items were donated back. Much of the castle has since been renovated. The grounds have shrunk over the centuries to only 20 hectares of rolling parkland, a formal terraced rose garden and an artificial lake that was added during the 19th century. Woodland pathways provide access to all the features in the park, including the small family burial ground.

Kilkenny Castle – the Long Gallery

Within the walls of the castle the exuberant spirit of the Victorian age has been re-created. In the Ante Room, Drawing Room and library, carpets woven to historic designs and walls hung with yellow silk are complemented by gilded pelmets and mahogany bookcases. The Long Gallery, the finest room in the house, has a striking 19th century hammer-beam and glass roof. An item that intrigued me was a shield on a pedestal in the drawing room. On enquiry, I was informed that it was a specially designed heat shield which was always placed in precisely the right position beside a lady of the house when she sat by the fire in order that her face did not become red from the heat of the fire. Ladies do *not* have red faces!

At the conclusion of our tour of the castle, we crossed the road to inspect the old stables. Before leaving Australia, my daughter Helena suggested I record not just what I saw, but also what I heard, smelt, tasted and felt. When we entered the main gate of the old stables, true to God, I heard the stamp of horses' hooves over the cobblestones – quite clearly, quite eerily! The stables are now an exhibition centre for local artists: pottery, jewellery, painters and the like.

We travelled south to visit to Jerpoint Abbey, two kilometres from the town of Thomastown, on the banks of the Little Arrigle River. It is one of the most interesting Cistercian ruins in Ireland. Founded in 1180 by the Cistercian monks from Baltinglass Abbey in Co. Wicklow, it was a daughter house of the first Irish Cistercian house in Mellifont in Co. Louth. The Cistercian order ('White Monks'), which was founded in France in 1098, followed an austere life of prayer and hard work. In 1217, disturbed by rumours of too much idle chatter, eating and drinking among the monks and lay-brothers and too much concern with personal belongings and contact with the outside world, the Cistercian General Chapter organised a general visitation and the abbot of Jerpoint was deposed for instigating the 'Riot of Jerpoint' in which four other Irish abbots were involved. This was part of a power struggle within the Cistercian Order between the Irish abbots and the Anglo-Norman abbots from Fountains Abbey in North Yorkshire which culminated in the 'Conspiracy of Mellifont' when all the Irish abbots were deposed. Jerpoint was taken from Baltinglass and made subject to Fountains, although its Irish affiliation was restored about fifty years later. Jerpoint continued to be the subject of debate which arose from continual accusations of its laxity in the strict Cistercian rule. At the time of the Dissolution of the Monasteries in 1540, the property was granted to James Butler, the Earl of Ormond. In the early years of the nineteenth century, the Cistercian ruins of Ireland became popular with the romantics. In 1823, the ruins evidently inspired a nostalgic poem, entitled 'Lines Written at Jerpoint Abbey'.

Jerpoint Abbey

One of the most outstanding features is the cloister arcade. The carvings on the pillars are still quite visible, ranging from human figures such as a bishop, a knight and his lady to grotesque and small unexpected figures in corners or on bases. In the ruins of the calefactory, we learned that it was here that the monks were allowed to speak – for ten minutes per day! It was also the only place in which the monks could heat themselves, again for ten minutes per day. Once a week the monks bled themselves of as much as eight pints as a form of penance. Conscious that water could carry disease, they did not drink water but were allowed to drink eight glasses of beer a day. It doesn't take too much of an imagination to see what bled, freezing monks were like after eight glasses of beer a day.

Cloister Arcade

Here, as with all the ruins and churches and abbeys, there are many tombs and gravesides in the grounds. Whilst burials in church grounds still continue in many places today, I learned a very interesting tale. In the centuries of the Penal Laws, designed to stamp out Catholicism, the Church went underground. Abbeys were pillaged and plundered by Cromwellian troops, and the people finished off much of the desecration. With no priest to pray over or bless the dead, the resident people went to abandoned abbeys, what they regarded as holy ground, dug up the floors and buried the bodies. Unfortunately, in doing so more damage was caused.

Abbeys were, as I am sure elsewhere in England and Europe, the hub of communal life. The people came to them for worship, albeit they were not allowed in the abbey and had to be content with watching Mass through the window for fear of corrupting the monks. To be sure, how could the abbot control fifty or so bleeding, freezing, eight-glass-a-day drinking monks from the venality of the freezing and starving local women or the envy of the beer famished men? Of course, the people were given permission to perform many tasks too menial for the holy men. But it did give the people opportunities to congregate.

A relief from castles, abbeys and ruins, we popped into nearby Mt. Juliet, a five-star golf course, and enjoyed a pint. The course had been designed by Jack Niclaus, the famous US golfer.

Something that intrigued and puzzled me was the huge number of elite golf courses in Ireland and the lack of public courses such as we have in Australia. It appeared that golf is a sport only for the rich! The few times Tom and I did have a game, it cost us between 40 and 50 Euros, whereas I could play 18 holes at my local public course in Australia for ten dollars.

On our return to Kilkenny, we visited the Dunmore Caves. Like all caves, they have stalagmites and stalactites and were huge. Whilst they were not as spectacular as the caves I have seen both in Western Australia and in New South Wales, what was of significance for me was their history. The caves were used by the Celts as hiding places from the ever-marauding Vikings. There is evidence in a cave of a monster massacre of women and children. The Vikings tried to flush them out by fire, thus killing the frightened, hiding Celts. Some years ago, Viking artefacts were found right up at the back of the cave, which is completely pitch black. The tour guide mentioned an interesting thing about the Vikings: they evidently did not carry bags or pouches on their clothing to store coins and such. Instead, they stuck the coins to their plentiful and thick body hair with a type of paste. Many of these were found on the cave floor.

Back to Kilkenny and a stroll through the town before a good meal and more cráic. We did not return to the pub of the night before: I did not want to disappoint the fellow in the band when he saw that I had not brought my bodhrán with me.

Filled with all that we had seen and experienced exploring Kilkenny City and its surrounds and tucked snugly in bed, I quickly fell asleep.

The words *'Hiems Transitt'* floated around me.

Nine

A highlight of our visit to Kilkenny was a tour of St. Kieran's where Tom studied for the priesthood. It is now a secondary college, an offshoot of Maynooth University.

We parked the car a short distance from the entrance. There it was, the sign I had longed to see: *Hiems Transitt*

When Tom finished his high schooling in Killarney in 1949, he was offered a scholarship in Cork University to study medicine. A condition of the scholarship was that, after graduation, he was to spend eight years in an African Mission. Although the opportunity to further his education appealed to him, the thought of all the blood and gore involved was not to his liking. He had thought he might like to study a branch of engineering as he had an aptitude for, and love of, mathematics. Unfortunately, his family did not have the money to pay for further education.

By this time, around 1949, his second eldest brother, John, and his younger brother, Jimmy, had immigrated to the United States. The oldest, Willie, was quite content to stay and work on the farm and it was traditionally assumed he would inherit the holding. Although Tom had loved growing up on the farm, he knew the life of a farmer was not for him. He did consider following John's footsteps to America and taking his chance at whatever the 'New World' had to offer.

Whilst sitting by a window and obviously day-dreaming one day, his mother said,

'Have you ever thought of being a priest?'

After admitting that he had thought about it, she simply replied, 'Well, why don't you do something about it?'

Years later, Tom often shared with me his wonder and awe in the way in which the God in whom he believed worked. Rarely did his God summon people with a thunderbolt in a call to them to enter religious life or the priesthood.

'It is usually in the quiet moments of stillness or through the gentle touch and interaction of another,' he firmly believed.

Tom was convinced it was through the example of the love and generosity and compassion for others, so much a part of his parents' characters that played a huge part in the eventual path he followed. 'I have no doubt,' he often declared, 'that my mother's gentle and loving care for me that day so long ago was the culmination of God's call to me.'

The next day, Tom called in to the presbytery in Kenmare and spoke to the curate, Father Michael Herlihy. A very matter-of-fact and down-to-earth man, the priest retorted after hearing the reason for his visit:

'Well, we have no room for you here in Ireland. After all, you didn't go to the Seminary in Killarney for your secondary education. You'll have to go overseas!'

Tom made a cursory remark that he may, possibly, apply to join a religious order; 'perhaps the Redemptorists?'

'For God's sake, keep away from them!' Fr. Herlihy thrust at Tom. He did tell Tom that one of Tom's neighbours, Fr. Jerry O'Farrell, was home on holidays from Australia and suggested Tom speak with him. 'They'll love you in Australia!' the curate quipped as he showed Tom to the door. *Did this imply there were not many priests in Australia?* Tom wondered. *What am I getting myself in for?*

However, Tom immediately jumped back on his bike and found Fr. Jerry out 'saving the hay' with his brothers. Following their conversation, Fr. Jerry wrote to Archbishop Prendiville in Perth and Tom did the same. A definite 'Yes!' was promptly returned. The die was cast. Tom was to study at St. Kieran's Seminary in Kilkenny which trained priests for countries outside of Ireland. Since it was late September, 1950 and the College year had already begun, Tom decided to wait till the new year before enrolling. He spent the time working on the farm, thinking and wondering and attempting to address his doubts and fears: *Could I do it? Would I be a good priest? Could I live my life as a celibate! Did I want to go to Australia?* He continued to say the prayer of his school days, *Thy will be done*, and by the end of the year, he was as ready as he thought he ever would be.

St. Kieran's was the first Catholic college opened in Ireland after the penal times, well before the other famous Ecclesiastical College at Maynooth. Above the portal of the college is written *Hiems Transitt,* Latin for 'Winter Has Passed.' During the college's construction in 1782, the people were celebrating the passing of the winter of persecution, the winter of the Penal Laws. At the time, in general they still smarted under the cruel and bitter rules and regulations of the Laws which affected the majority Catholic population of Ireland. The building of St. Kieran's College was the first gleam of light at the end of a long and painful tunnel.

During the first couple of years at St.Kieran's, Tom found it very difficult. He had never lived away from home and the discipline of institutional life was hard to bear. He questioned his vocation, being thrown into areas of study that were completely foreign to him. With the constant challenges faced from superiors, spiritual advisors and lecturers, he became more aware of his own human failings and difficulties. He despaired of ever achieving the high standard of spirituality promoted in the college. He had always enjoyed the company of women, and had strong sexual desires. He mentioned his fears to one of the spiritual directors and was told not to worry about it, to keep up his prayers and continue with his studies.

'Every priest feels that way', Tom was told. 'That's what makes a good priest.' Tom wondered what the hell that meant! The director then questioned Tom on his vocation, what had led him to St. Kieran's, what were his motives. His answer was simple:

'To do good, to spread the Word and to help people.' Tom was assured that his vocation appeared valid. He pressed on.

Elocution took up a large part of the curriculum in that first year. There were candidates for the Priesthood from all parts of Ireland and it was a veritable tower of Babel with all the different dialects. Since they were destined for various countries around the world, the young seminarians spent many hours preparing for the time when they would eventually be preaching. Each night, they would proceed to a large hall in the lay wing of the college. They would stand at one end of the hall and read certain passages, attempting to throw their voices and improve their pronunciation.

This, that, these and those! The words tormented Tom, and others like him, who had come from the south of Ireland. During one rehearsal period, a fellow Kerryman was asked to recite a phrase for the class. He had to say: *Boiling oil for toil*. Try and get a Kerry accent round that! It came out more like: *Biling ile for tile*. Being close to the end of the session, the elocution teacher said, *Oh sir, I think by now you're more interested in biling tay*!

From time to time, the lads from the distant counties would receive parcels from home; these were eagerly awaited. They invariably contained biscuits and home-baked cakes and such other delicacies. At one time, a pound of butter – an absolute luxury – was sent to Tom from Kenmare. He had to pick it up from the special place in the refectory before lunch, and after lunch, he went outside for some fresh air and put the pound of butter on top of a gate pillar. Hallway during the afternoon study-break, he remembered his pound of butter on the gate. He ran down the corridor and stairs, his soutane flapping, only to bump smack into the Dean, who was sedately strolling along as he recited his Office. The Dean promptly started to lecture Tom on the inappropriateness of his behaviour and that he should not be tearing around the place and to forget the butter. Tom tried to remain calm, his feet shifting from one to the other, his thoughts, of course, only on the butter. After more admonitions, the Dean let him go. At last, Tom was freed to regain his butter.

In his later years, Tom often spoke of the grief he realised in the lack of a broad education during his six years at St. Kieran's. Their reading was strictly controlled. A forbidden copy of the daily newspaper was smuggled into the college by the local shoemaker. He would come to collect shoes to be repaired and meet the guys from 4th Year of Divinity or Theology and pass on the contraband, which would then be hidden under the soutane and slowly passed down the ranks. By the time the paper reached the 1st year Philosophy students, the paper would be at least a week old. The college library was bereft of any novels or other pieces of like literature. Catholic papers from other dioceses throughout the world were the only permissible periodicals allowed to be read. The occasional football match was the only radio broadcast permitted. Surrounded by very high walls, the seminarians were not allowed to look over the walls – a rule extremely difficult to regulate! Tom did acknowledge that this was the thinking of the times: the students had to be protected from the perverse 'outer world' in case their vocation received a beating. This did not prepare the young men for the outer world.

The only permitted reading was the set syllabus for each subject in the curriculum. Although being prepared for the world Mission Field, they were not taught any other language: supposedly they were prepared to be disciplined, obedient Holy Men of the Church, intellectually starved at a time in life when their brains were like sponges. Their humanity and individuality got a bashing and for many this proved detrimental, if not fatal. Although pastoral theology was part of the syllabus, curriculum and guided to lead a life of service to 'ordinary' people, they were not tutored in anything pertaining to ordinary people's complex lives. Schooled to live a life of celibacy, a promise that was to be made prior to ordination, they were not taught anything about the wonder and beauty of human sexuality; hence, an appreciation of what that commitment involved was limited.

Tom came to understand why so many priests left active ministry in the decades immediately following the Second Vatican Council in the early 1960s. Communication and conflict resolution proficiency and anger management strategies, imperative skills Tom believed every priest should be taught, have only become part of the over-all education and formation reflected in the Church of the modern epoch. In the years prior to Vatican II, the priest was seen to be 'above' ordinary life; he was different, sacred, a holy man of God. He did not need to know how mundane people lived. Should he be surprised, Tom often bemoaned, at the scandals that have rocked the Church?

Tom and his classmates of the previous six years were ordained on Sunday, 2nd June 1957. With mixed feelings, they said their goodbyes, all of them to be dispersed to the four corners of the globe. Following a holiday in Kenmare, Tom left for Australia in mid-September, 1957. His father having died the year previously, Tom found it extremely hard to say goodbye to his mother. After a long hug and kiss, he ran out of the house, daring not to look back. His brother Willie took him to Cove, about 40 kilometres from Kenmare. Although sad to be leaving his mother and brother and friends, Tom was also filled with a great sense of excited expectation of the life and journey ahead. His old familiar doubts also surfaced occasionally: *Will I make it?*

St.Kieran's college
This Photo by Unknown Author is licensed under CC BY-SA

At the celebratory Mass at the time of Tom's 40th Anniversary of his Ordination, it was my privilege to give a short address:

'It gives me great pleasure to pay tribute to Fr. Tom on the occasion of his 40th Anniversary of his Ordination. In order to do this, I would like to draw some parallels to the Celtic Church and the ancient tradition into which he was born.

'The Celtic Church put its anchor deep into the Word of God. Their Faith was so rooted in the Scriptures that they carried it in their memory, reciting Psalms as they walked the muddied pathways. In the Psalms, the Celts found a mirror image for their abiding love for all Creation. They had a tremendous depth of spiritual life and a love for stillness. In the stillness, reflecting on Creation, they found God.

'Columba, one of the great Saints of the Celtic Church, wrote:

> *Delightful it is to stand on the peak of a rock,*
> *in the bosom of the isle, gazing on the face of the sea.*
> *I hear the heaving waves chanting a tune to God in heaven;*
> *I see the golden beaches, their sands sparkling;*

I hear the waves breaking, crashing on rocks,
like thunder in heaven.
Contrition fills my heart as I hear the sea; it chants my sins.
I pray for peace, kneeling at heaven's gates.
Delightful it is to live on a peaceful isle, in a quiet cell,
serving the King of Kings.

'The Celts were a prayerful people and their prayers were always deeply Trinitarian. Celtic Christians found it as natural to pray during the milking of a cow as they did in Church. They ardently believed in their responsibility to use intercessory prayer to heal the rifts in God's creation brought about by sin. The Celtic Church was all too aware of the damage done to creation by sin and so they had a great love for the Cross. You can still see today in Ireland many examples of the huge standing cross, planted firmly in the soil, as a sign of Christ's redeeming work in the heart of God's good, but damaged, creation. To turn a battle site into a place of prayer was typical of the Celtic desire to heal the land, to turn darkness into light. And this became hallowed ground.

'Their lives were utterly given to mission. They delighted in allowing the Wild Geese to take them to un-evangelized places with the good news of Jesus. They had a radical commitment to the poor. Columba prayed:

Let me do my daily work, gathering seaweed,
catching fish, giving to the poor.
Let me say my daily prayers, sometimes chanting,
sometimes quiet, always thanking God.

'Influenced by their love of the Trinity, we find in the Celtic Church a strong community context in which men and women worked happily together. For them, the Father, Son and Holy

Spirit existed in perfect community and, therefore, the Church needed to express this community life while it sought to serve the God who is Three. The Celtic Church accepted and embraced the feminine coupled with a deep reverence for the miraculous. They found great joy in a faith filled with creative life, a faith that affirmed their inherent delight in music, poetry and art.

'The Celts were an adventurous people yet rich in simplicity. They were a people whose hearts were gloriously set on heaven while their feet were firmly planted in the soil: loving creation, caring for it and seeing through it the work of God and through which they could answer the call, *Come, follow Me*.

'Today we have gathered together to celebrate with another Celtic son, Thomas Columba Gaine. Forty years ago, Fr. Tom left the country of his birth, a country he loved, in his attempt to answer the call, *Come, follow Me*. He left his mother and brothers, his friends and loved ones, to journey to a strange land. All he had with him was a deep and abiding love for his God and an utter and complete trust and faith that the hand of God would guide him. In his own inimitable way, he has shared with us today some of his early experiences in that new land.

'He soon came to love his new country with its wide and open spaces, its golden beaches and sparkling seas, developing a deep respect for the land of the Great Spirit. Like his namesake of long ago, he has an adventurous spirit and eagerly set his hand to the plough God had handed him. As he moved from parish to parish with his typical openness to life and exuberance and love of his God, he quickly endeared himself to young and old alike. Although he became known for calling a spade a spade, he is also loved for his willingness and readiness to accept people as they were, neither condemning nor judging but always ready to share with them his love for

God and his love of life.

'We are happy to have this chance to thank you, Fr. Tom, for your authenticity, for being the person and priest that you are; for your dedication and faithfulness to your priesthood. Thank you for sharing with us your love of your God, your love of the Mass and the healing power of the Sacraments in a way that speaks to us in a language we understand and helping us to find God in our human experiences.

'We want to thank you for sharing with us your wonder and awe of God's Creation, for your deep and abiding love of the Scriptures, for your reverence for silence and your willingness to listen to God in the depths of your heart. We want to thank you for your sense of justice, for your love of the poor and your great generosity. For your respect for and love of all people.

'Thank you for sitting with us in our kitchens, celebrating with us in times of gladness and weeping with us in times of sorrow. Thank you for the respect you show for our own worth and giving us opportunities to discern our own giftedness.

'Thank you for your humanity and your humility and for the courage you show in allowing us to see your own limitations and your own idiosyncrasies, your funny little ways that sometimes drive us up the wall but that we have, nevertheless, grown to love. And thank you for accepting our own.

'And thank you for teaching us to pray, over and over again, *Thank you Lord.*'

Of course, much of the college is now changed. But Tom was able to show me his old dormitory, classrooms, chapel, refectory.

'See over there,' Tom said as we walked through the gardens, 'that's where I left my precious pound of butter!'

Tom expressed his grave disappointment at the alterations undertaken to the Catholic cathedral in which he was ordained. Since Vatican II, a major part of the high altar had been brought forward and two thirds of the Cathedral is now taken up with the Sanctuary, leaving very little room for the people, as pews are crammed up one upon the other.

St Canice's Protestant Cathedral – originally Catholic – on the other hand was magnificent with lots of room for the people. The hilltop cathedral, flanked by a round tower, was built in the 13th century in Early Gothic Style on the ruins of an ancient Celtic church. The 100-foot tower was built around 849 as hiding places from the Vikings. The view from the top of the tower delivered a wonderful view of the city: its many historic buildings, the *slips*, the pubs, the variety of colours.

The cathedral was sacked by Cromwell's forces in 1650. He used the cathedral to stable his horses, smashed the front windows and threw out the tombs and monuments. Throughout all my touring of Ireland I was continually confronted by the extent of the destruction Cromwell caused in his determination to rid Ireland of all things Catholic. Fortunately, the church was restored and is now one of Ireland's greatest medieval treasures. An array of some of the tombs that survived Cromwell's desecration include beautiful effigies of the Butler family in the south transept.

Near St. Canice's is the Black Abbey, a Dominican Abbey founded in 1225. Also violated by Cromwell, it was turned into a courthouse in the 16th century. It is once again a working monastery, boasts a fine vaulted undercroft and some beautiful stained-glass windows which date back to the 14th century.

I was flabbergasted to learn that Kilkenny has four Catholic parishes!

Delightfully swamped by cathedrals, churches, beautiful windows, magnificent restorations, I turned to Tom and said,

'Don't you think we have earned a pint and a bite to eat?'

Settled comfortably with pint in hand, I wandered back in memory to our tour of St.Kieran's. I looked toward my old friend, thought back over the years we had worked together, the challenges faced together, the friendship formed. Pictured him nearly fifty years ago boarding the boat at Cove, setting out for the Great South Land, full of enthusiasm and belief in the God of his ancestors. A journey to a land so inexorably linked to the land of his birth, a land which, to a large extent, had fashioned his manhood.

I raised my glass, whispered: *Yes, friend, you did indeed make it.*

The next day, the weather had cleared so we headed back to Cashel in Co. Tipperary, famous for the Rock of Cashel. The rocky stronghold – an ancient symbol of royal and priestly power for more than a millennium – rises dramatically out of a Tipperary plain, overlooking the Golden Veil. From the 5th century, it was the seat of the Munster kings, whose kingdom extended over much of southern Ireland. In 1101, it was handed over to the Church and it flourished as a religious centre until a siege by a Cromwellian army in 1647, which resulted in the massacre of its 3000 inhabitants. The cathedral was finally abandoned in the late 18th century. Two hundred years on and the Rock of Cashel is besieged yet again, this time by thousands of visitors.

Rock of Cashell

Tradition tells that King Conall Corc was baptized at the Rock by Patrick, who visited the Rock in 450. In a burst of fervour during the ceremony, Patrick thrust his sharply pointed crozier down and pierced the foot of the king, who, believing it to be a part of the ritual, suffered in silence.

The rock is full of ancient features. There is a 28 metre tall tower which, it is said, enabled the inhabitants of Cashel to scour the surrounding plain for potential attackers. The Choir contains the 17th century tomb of Miler Magrath who caused a scandal by being both a Protestant and a Catholic archbishop for nine years! Magrath was ordained a Franciscan priest who spent his early life in Rome. On his return to Ireland in 1565, he was appointed Catholic Bishop of Down and Connor. In 1567, he agreed to conform to the reformed faith and appointed Protestant Bishop of Down and Connor in 1569 whilst at the same time, held on to the Catholic See. In 1580, he was deposed by Rome for heresy.

St. Patrick's Cross is a copy of the original which stood on the Rock until 1982 and which is said to have on its east face a carving of Patrick; the original is now in the museum. In the undercroft, the museum contains a large display of stone carvings. Cormac's Chapel with its superb Romanesque carvings, known as the Jewel of Cashel, has a door which shows a centaur in a helmet aiming his bow and arrow at a lion; this is believed to be an example of the strong influence of the Scandinavian Urnes, the last stage of Scandinavian art during the second half of the 11th century and first half of the 12th century.

And so our fabulous week came to a close. We steered clear of Limerick City as that was where George W. Bush was due to arrive the next day.

A site of interest on the way back to Lissyclerig was yet another ruin. Compelled to stop, I examined the gravestones. One in particular was striking. The grave was that of Thomas Brennan, 42 years, his wife, 40 years and three sons, 21, 20 and 18 years – dated 1857 – all victims of the famine. It was a strange experience to see and hear the name Brennan so often.

The tombstone was erected by a daughter, Jessie Jacobs, of New York. Jacobs is evidently a common Quaker name. The American Quakers did much to help the victims of the famine. Did the daughter escape the famine years? Did she emigrate to America and marry a Quaker? Or did she marry prior to leaving Ireland?

As we drove back towards Kerry, I pondered on all we had seen, all that I had felt, heard, smelt. History dating back 1500 years! Goodness, I thought, the oldest places we have in Australia are, what, 200 years?

'Stop the car, Tom!'

I stepped from the car, looked all around me. The stillness, the quietness, held me in a trance. What was I saying to myself – Australia only has 200 years of history? Aboriginal and Torres Strait Islander people have been in Australia for more than 40,000 years! Australia *does* have a history! Okay, it might not be recorded history in the Western view of history, but history it still is. Surely?

I re-entered the car; Tom drove on. The silence continued.

Yes, the *presence* assured me. Australia does have a history. But is it the history of *my* ancient soul? Is it a history I can relate to? Is it a history that has meaning in my life? Were there even more questions that had not yet been given a voice?

Our temples are built in the ground.
Our castles are in the dirt.
We ourselves are written in the stars.

From The Shadow King
Tom E. Lewis

Ten

The Ring of Kerry is a stunning coastal ring route around the Iveragh Peninsular in Co. Kerry and a national natural treasure. Its official start and finish is Killarney and, while most tourist buses would travel in an anti-clockwise direction, it can be travelled in either direction. The south coast of the peninsular runs along the north side of Kenmare Bay. We commenced our travels from Kenmare and travelled clockwise.

The first town we drove through was Sneem. Brightly coloured red, green and yellow cottages line the streets of this charming town. We stopped for a morning cuppa in a café overlooking the quaint village green.

Our next stop was Staigue Fort. Set on a hill up a narrow track, this Iron Age dry stone fort – *caheh* – is the best preserved in Ireland. The walls are almost five and a half metres high and four metres wide and about 27.4 metres in diameter. What amazed me was that the fort – and many other similar buildings – was built without any mortar. The stones were cut and placed in such a precise manner that no wind or rain could destroy it. There is much debate as to how old the fort is – but a consensus suggests that Staigue Fort has been there for about 2000 years. It has sweeping views of the valley and the mouth of the Kenmare River and sea beyond. A fort of such size, undoubtedly, would have been the domain of a wealthy Celtic leader and his clan. The compound would have held about five or six huts with plenty of space for sheep and cattle. Its strategic position offered a wide, clear view of the neighbouring countryside and afforded ample protection from marauding tribes.

Staigue Fort

What little is known of pre-Christian Ireland comes from a few references in Roman writings, Irish poetry and myth, and archaeology. The earliest inhabitants of Ireland, hunter-gatherers from Britain and continental Europe, of a mid-Stone or Mesolithic Age, probably arrived via a land bridge sometime after 8000 BC, when the climate had become more hospitable following the retreat of the polar icecaps. About 4000 BC agriculture was introduced from the Continent, leading to the establishment of a high Neolithic culture, characterized by the appearance of pottery, polished stone tools, rectangular wooden houses and communal megalithic tombs, as seen in such sites as Newgrange. It was towards the end of the Neolithic age that new types of monuments developed, such as circular embanked enclosures and pit circles as seen in Staigue Fort.

The Bronze Age began once copper was alloyed with tin to produce true bronze artefacts around 2000 BC. There was a movement away from the construction of communal megalithic tombs to the burial of the dead in small stone cists or simple pits, which could be situated in cemeteries or in circular earth or stone built mounds known respectively as barrows and cairns. As the period progressed, inhumation burial gave way to cremation and by the Middle Bronze Age cremations were often placed beneath large burial urns.

As the Bronze Age in Ireland drew to a close, there appeared in Ireland a new cultural influence. Developing in the Alps of central Europe, the Celts spread their culture across modern-day Germany and France and into the Balkans as far as Turkey. Whether or not the arrival of the Celts in Ireland was an actual invasion, or a more gradual assimilation, is an open question. On the one hand, the Celts – who were by no means pacifists – must have arrived in sufficiently large numbers to obliterate the existing culture in Ireland within a few hundred years. On the other hand, other better documented invasions of Ireland – such as the Viking invasions of the 7th and 8th centuries AD – failed to have the effect of changing the culture on an island-wide scale. Current academic opinion favours the theory that the Celts arrived over several centuries, beginning in the late Bronze Age with the Celts of the early iron-using Hallstatt group of people, to be followed after 300 BC by Celts of La Tène cultural group which formed within the Hallstatt group.

The medieval 'Book of Invasions', otherwise known as *Lebor Gabála Érenn*, is purported to be a literal and accurate account of the history of the Irish and could be seen as an attempt to deliver the Irish a written history comparable to that which the Israelites provided for themselves in the Old Testament. Biblical paradigms offered the mythologists ready-made stories which could be adapted to their purpose. Thus we see the ancestors of Ireland enslaved in a foreign land, or fleeing into exile, or wandering in the wilderness, or sighting the 'Promised Land'.

Numerous fragments of Irish legendary history are scattered throughout the 7th and 8th centuries. The earliest extant account, which comprises two separate accounts of early Irish history, was written by a Welsh priest Nennius in 829-830 called *Historia Brittonum* or 'History of the Britons'. It was late in the 11th century that a single anonymous scholar appears to have brought together the two stories written by Nannius and plentiful other poems and legends and compiled them into an elaborate prose framework – partly of his own composition and partly drawn from older, no longer extant sources. The result was the earliest version of *Lebor Gabála Èrenn*.

Some have postulated that, as the Romans invaded and took control of the continental Celtic territories of Gaul [France] and Iberia [Spain and Portugal], some of the displaced Celts travelled to unconquered Celtic lands such as Britain and Ireland. The 'Book of Invasions' talks about *Milesians* and *Fír Bolg* arriving in Ireland. These have been identified with displaced Celts from Spain and Belgium, respectively, although this is conjecture.

In whatever way the Celts arrived in Ireland, within a few hundred years, Ireland's Bronze Age culture had all but disappeared, and Celtic culture was in place across the entire island. The Celts had one major advantage – they had discovered iron. Iron had been introduced to the Celtic peoples in Europe around 1000 to 700BC, thus giving them the technological edge to spread as they did. Iron was a far superior metal to bronze, being stronger and more durable. On the other hand, it required much hotter fires to extract it from its ore and so it took a fair degree of skill to use iron. None of this, evidently, is to be taken to mean that bronze fell out of use. Rather, iron simply became an alternative metal and many bronze objects have been found that were made in the Iron Age.

I rubbed my hands along the stone wall with amazement at the engineering feat of an ancient people, and my imagination danced a wild jig. I heard the bleating of the sheep, the soft, melodious lowing of cattle. I heard the joyful chatter as the women went about their daily chores, the laughter of many children. I saw the men return at day's end as they shepherded their flocks into the fort after a day of grazing on the near-by hillside. I heard the music and songs as night fell.

Transported back to eons past, I also could not help but recall how my *presence* assured me that the indigenous people of the land of my birth did indeed have the oldest history of civilisation on earth. But Australia is such an isolated country. It was not invaded till the 18th Century and when it did happen, the invaders were not at all interested in discovering or learning of any 'living history', of searching the depths of myth and art. To be sure, wasn't this land called *Terra Nullius?* What grave injustice has been perpetuated on both the original inhabitants of this land and those of us who are descendants of the invaders that the history of this incredible country has not been valued and cherished?

As we continued our drive west along the Ring of Kerry and passed the numerous buses filled with tourists, I thought of the Great Ocean Road in Victoria and its beauty.

'Stop the car, Tom!' I cried out. 'This reminds me of Australia. I need a swim.' Thankfully, I had packed my bathers. Tom found a lovely cove at which there were a number of people enjoying the warm weather. I changed and plunged into the Atlantic Ocean.

'Go on,' Tom says. 'Show them how they swim in Australia.' How I wished I had my snorkel and goggles with me!

As the road began to swerve north, we passed through

Caherdaniel, the birth place of Daniel O'Connell, the 'Liberator', famous for his tireless work to free the Irish from British rule in the late 1700s and early 1800s. The former home of O'Conell, Derrynane House, now houses a museum featuring his memorabilia. As I looked out upon the rugged Atlantic coastline, I understood how easy it must have been for the many members of the O'Conell family to pirate guns into Ireland at this point.

Caherdaniel - Ring of Kerry

Our next stop was at Waterville, which, at its entry, there is a park that holds a statue of Charlie Chaplin. Chaplin's wife was Oonagh O'Neill, the daughter of the playwright Eugene O'Neill who wrote the Playboy of the Western World. Chaplin's daughter, Josephine, lived near Waterville and Chaplin visited this part of Kerry every year for a holiday.

Further north we arrived at Caherciveen, the main town on the peninsular and home to a local heritage centre. A huge cathedral-like church dedicated to O'Connor was in the middle of the town. Throughout all my travels, I was always stunned by the size of the churches, even in such small towns as Caherciveen. I could not help but think they must have been a testament to the degree of hope they offered in the dark days of the past. Following our visit to the centre, we decided to stay the night in the town.

During our evening meal, Tom told me the story of how, in his teens, he spent a couple of weeks in Waterville teaching young people Irish. Since he has been back in Ireland over the last three years, he has managed to pick up more Irish that he had lost over the previous 45 years or so in Australia. Evidently many young people today learn Irish and spend a couple weeks each summer and travel to a *Ghaeltact* – Irish-speaking – area such as Dingle and board with a local family who only speak Irish. I think it is fantastic that obvious efforts are being made to foster and encourage the Irish language.

It never ceased to amaze me the large number of B&Bs throughout the country; the owners were always so friendly and hospitable and the service was excellent. After a scrumptious breakfast – which was always supplied by the owners of the B&Bs in which we stayed – of fruit and crunchy cereal followed by a large serve of fried black pudding, bacon, eggs and grilled tomato, we headed off to Portmagee and Valentia Island to board a boat out to the Skellig Islands which are 12 kilometres south west of Valentia. Skellig Michael – also known as Great Skellig – and Small Skellig, like two fairy tale castles, rise defiantly from the sea, two mountains of rock. The name derives from *Sceillic*, which means a steep rock. The first reference to the Skelligs occurs in legend when it is given as the burial place of Ir, son of Milesius, who was drowned during the landing of the Milesians.

Skellig Michael rises 218 metres above sea level and drops to 50 metres below the sea, providing an aquatic playground for giant basking sharks, dolphins and turtles. It covers an area of 17 ha. From the boat, I gazed with awe at the two majestic sentinels, silent witnesses to many aspects of Irish maritime history. Perched on the top of the main island, and reached by an amazing 1000 year old stairway, is an isolated early Christian Monastery said to be founded by St. Fionán during the 6th century. However, tradition is resorted to for 'proof' of the monastery's founder as there may have been two St. Fionáns: St. Fionán the Squint-Eyed and St. Fionán the Leper. Fionán is an Irish name meaning 'the fair-headed one' and there were a number of Fionáns. St Aidan's successor at Lindisfarne was called Fionán, and there was 'Fionán Cam', 'Cam' meaning that he had a squint, from Kerry. *Lobhar* (sometimes written *lobur*) is an Irish word meaning a leper or someone suffering from a chronic skin disease.

Buffeted by strong Atlantic storms, the monks survived and built six corbelled beehive cells and two boat-shaped oratories. These dry-stone structures still stand, despite being raked by centuries of storms. The monks were totally self-sufficient, trading eggs, feathers and seal meat with passing boats in return for cereals, tools and animal skins. The skins were needed to produce the vellum on which the monks copied their religious manuscripts. It was not till the 11th century when the European Orders of Benedictines and Augustinians were invited to Ireland that the independent heritages came to an end. At least 23 other islands off the west coast of Ireland have monastic ruins, with Skellig Michael claiming the finest example of early Christian architecture. The monks remained on the island until the 12th century when they retreated to the Augustinian priory at Ballinskelligs on the mainland, after bombardment by the Vikings forced them to relinquish their island home.

As the boat circled Small Skellig, the rocky island appeared to be covered in a flowing white veil. In and around every crevice – soaring, diving, teeming, screaming – 29,000 pairs of goose-sized gannets jostled for nesting space with thousands of storm petrels, puffins, Manx shearwaters and other sea-birds. Unseen, but certainly not un-heard, the night-time cry of the shearwaters is the most unnerving sound on the Atlantic Ocean. Except for a pier on Skellig Michael, there are no proper landing stages on the islands. This is to discourage visitors from disturbing the birdlife, fragile plant cover and archaeological remains. At any given moment in summer, 100,000 birds make Small Skellig their home.

Small Skellig

Well, gidday, all you white fellas. Come 'ere, I'll tell ye how we and our ancestors, the Bardi people, come to know about the birds that fill up the skies here in the north of Western Australia. In the very early days of the Alcheringa – what you white fellas call the Dreaming – when the Great Spirit created birds, they was black – plain black!

One bright, sunny mornin', a dove flew around lookin' for food. The little bird spotted a worm and he, well he dived to snatch it from a hole in a log. When he landed, he pricked his foot on a sharp splinter. The wound started to bleed, and the bird fell down and rolled onto his back.

Soon, birds of many kinds swooped down. They gathered round the little bird, anxious to help. Some dropped water in the wounded bird's mouth. Others washed the wound and tried to stop the bleedin' with leaves. Some flew overhead, protectin' the little bird from the harsh sun. They wondered what else they could do to help the little bird from its sufferin'.

All of 'em, except the crow.

The big black crow strutted round like he was king. He ordered all the birds to go and mind their own business. The flutterin' of wings, the flyin' to and fro, and their loud chatter disturbed his peace and quiet. He fluffed his feathers, flapped his wings and shrieked with anger. The frightened birds scattered but still hovered close by. They was upset about the little bird. Its foot got worse and swelled to three times its normal size.

A galah, known for her quick thinkin', as well as her sharp beak, flew down to the dyin' bird. The other birds watched in horror as she pecked at the injured foot. The little bird cried out in terrible pain. The birds thought lots of pus, dried blood and other stuff would ooze out of the wound.

But magically, a great stream of magnificent colours shot out from the wound. The colours dripped onto the amazed birds. Splashes of pink, light grey and pure white fell onto the galah. She shrieked with delight, danced about, and admired herself. Spurts of yellow, purple, blue, green and red fell onto the other birds. They was all so excited.

Some birds was drenched with jus' one colour. Others was spotted with many colours. The lorikeets looked like a whole flamin' rainbow. The little bird, who was now a lovely, pure white, well she danced with joy.

It was a very special day for all the birds. They knew they'd

be able to keep their new and beautiful colours for ever.
And that is how the birds are all different colours.

The Bardi People,
Broome, Western Australia
Rainbow Coloured Birds, Jean A. Ellis

On our arrival back at Valentia, we explored the Skellig Experience Centre which houses audio-visual displays about the construction and history of the monastery on Skellig Michael and information on the birds and marine life of the islands.

Although it feels like the mainland, Valentia is an island, linked by a causeway to Portmagee. The first transatlantic cable was laid from the southwest point of the island to Newfoundland, Canada, in 1866. The main village on Valentia is Knightstown which offers accommodation and lively pubs with music and dancing. Although it was a bit early in the day to enjoy much dancing, we did relish a hearty meal and a pint or two. After driving around Portmagee, we headed back to Caherciveen and east to Killorglin and booked into a B&B, and then enjoyed another fabulous meal of salmon.

After breakfast, we continued to head east towards Killarney and detoured to see some old Ogham Stones.

Ogham is the earliest form of Celtic writing which flourished from the 4th to 7th centuries. It takes its name from Ogma, the Celtic god of eloquence and literature. These early markings were either carved on wood or stone, although the stones are the only surviving examples. The stones were usually placed in a strategic spot in remembrance of a memorable event or person and also as boundary markers. The majority of the remaining stones, between two and three metres high are to be found in Kerry.

The Ogham alphabet, symbols named after trees and plants, consist of a series of twenty-five perpendicular or angled strokes marked either side or across a line with the edge of the stone the centre line. They are read from bottom up, across the top of the stone and, when necessary, down the other side. A single stroke across the line is equivalent to the Latin letter A, the letter B a single stroke on the right hand side whilst C is represented by four strokes on the left side.

The early Christian missionaries discouraged and later forbade their use because of a mistaken belief that the stones were employed in Druidic pagan rituals.

Ogham Stone

I was struck by the similarities between the marks on the stones and the strokes and dots found in Pittman shorthand.

At age 15, a week or two before the end of the school year, I was summoned into my father's den.

'Elizabeth.' The tone of his voice alerted me: this was serious! 'Your Aunt Joan (Dad's sister) and I have decided that you will leave school and study to become a secretary. You are enrolled in a nine-month Secretarial Course at North Sydney Tech.'

End of conversation. Summarily dismissed, I sought out my mother. She could not help me. I had just completed the Intermediate Certificate – equivalent to today's Year 10 – and looked forward to another two years at school at the end of which I would sit for my Matriculation. Wasn't there plenty of time to think about a career, faith?

I finished the course at North Sydney Tech.: learned how to type, mastered shorthand, achieved the desired 100 words per minute, was introduced to book-keeping and the intricacies of Commercial English. At the end of the year, I was summoned yet again to my father's presence. I was informed of another of his and Aunt Joan's decisions: I was to commence employment the following Monday as a stenographer at Newnham and Newnham, Solicitors, in Martin Place, Sydney. This time my mother had also received her orders: the next day she bought me a black skirt and white blouse. And sensible shoes.

In Western Australia, the Burrup Peninsular, 28 kilometres northwest of Karratha, catastrophe is being perpetrated.

The area has been described as the world's largest art gallery: hundreds of standing stones, dating back 20,000 years, are being destroyed by development and mining. Archaeologists attest that the stones point to significant human habitation in the Burrup.

Some stand alone, others are clustered in groups. The Burrup is home to Australia's biggest collection of standing stones, some up to two metres high. More than 3000 have already been destroyed.

Hundreds of thousands of Aboriginal petroglyphs (rock engravings) are distributed over an area of 88 sq. kilometres. They range from small engravings of emu tracks to very large ones representing some kind of corroboree or ceremony. They depict a Tasmanian tiger, whales, kangaroos, emus and thousands of Aboriginal ceremonies.

But, sadly, the people are long gone. The invaders of this land were not interested in discovering the meaning of these symbols of an ancient culture. They refused to believe that such a culture existed before their arrival. No one will ever know what the engravings really represent. The Jaburara people who once lived here have been wiped out.

For a long time, the West Australian Government, along with Woodside Energy Ltd., opposed a heritage listing of this 'prehistoric university'. It was claimed that heritage listing of the area would be an 'economic catastrophe' and any heritage listing would not go ahead without concessions to the energy sector. When the Federal Government announced National Heritage listing for the Burrup Peninsular on 3 July, 2007, it explicitly excluded the Woodside lease.

But, faith, why do we worry about such things? We need only hop on a plane and go to Ireland to see ancient art in the Ogham Stones in Co. Kerry. What's the big deal?

The Gap of Dunloe, hewn two million years ago by giant, slow moving ice is probably the finest example of a glaciated valley in Western Europe. The Gap has long been a popular tourist attraction. The road through it is narrow, winding and difficult for larger vehicles. A popular form of transport for tourists is the horse-drawn trap, a cart where up to four occupants sit facing each other. There are also riding ponies for hire. The trap and ponies are guided by men from families that live in and around the Gap. These pony-men use a rotation system called the Turn which determines who takes the next customers. The Turn has been in existence since the 1920s and is passed down in the families to the next generation.

The road through The Gap is begun from a popular starting point, Kate Kearney's Cottage and winds down to Lord Brandon's Cottage, from where you can get a boat back to Killarney; it is about 11 kilometres long, climbing and descending about 200 meters altogether. We parked the car, donned our walking shoes, and ensured enough water and fruit were in our back packs.

'Enjoy your walk. Great weather. Best summer we've ever had.'

We set off. It took about two hours to walk the length.

The landscape in the Gap and, indeed, in the adjacent Lakes of Killarney, owes its beauty to the glaciers of the last Ice Age over a million years ago. Twenty thousand years ago, as the ice shrank backwards, it scooped out three deep lakes. The Upper Lake was literally gouged out, whilst the Middle and Lower Lakes were formed by the layers of limestone that had lain beneath the ice dissolving in the thaw. Elsewhere, the glaciers left debris in the wake such as at the Gap of Dunloe and wore away gigantic boulders and rocks at Moll's Gap, on the Killarney/Kenmare Road. Today the mountains are covered in purple heathers and boast a quarter of all the rare Irish plants. From May to July the hillsides and damper areas yield many Mediterranean-Lusitanian plants such as Butterworts and Saxifrages, while in July and August American oddities such as blue-eyed grasses and unusual rushes appear.

Gap of Dunloe

It was a popular destination for walkers, and we encountered people from many different countries. Of its very nature, however, the Gap invites solitude; I was content to acquiesce, set my own pace, happy for Tom to walk on ahead. I had no need for conversation. Ah, the mountains! I craned my neck upwards, sideways, allowed myself to be saturated. What need of cathedrals? Yes, I could hear my kids say, when I was to tell them about our hike: 'Here's Mum. Going off about mountains … again!' The mountains rise steeply, almost perpendicularly, from both sides of the walk

Every now and then, on the side of the road, we passed an abandoned stone house. There would probably have been half a dozen or so families living in the Gap of old, farming and tending their sheep on the mountain slopes. When I reached the second such cottage, I sat down on the grass-covered stone-wall surrounding the ruins. The road had become quite steep. I retrieved my water bottle and drank deeply.

As I sat and rested, the house spoke; I mouthed a reply …

You stand, disabled, defiant. Wait patiently for the storm, knowing that it will pass. Assured that when the wind wrestles with you, you will not be defeated. Your thatched roof has long since succumbed to countless storms, raging winds of long ago. Your empty, cavernous heart, now outwardly silenced, beckons all with ears to hear.

Your solid, aged stone-walls, now only a semblance of past beauty, hold deep memories of yesteryear. Of nights when they reverberated with the songs of neighbours and friends, congregated in the long winter evenings around a blazing turf, their laughter and banter ricocheting in and around you. When your earthen floors were swept by eager dancing feet, mesmerised by the pulsating rhythm of a bodhrán and the lilting music of a lone tin whistle. Of times when your walls wept and blended with the women's creening in times of sorrow. How they flexed and bent to accommodate the arrival and cry of yet another new born, another mouth to feed.

Today you are isolated but never alone.

Your ruins are surrounded by damp, moss-covered, low stone-walls that have weathered the passing of time despite being built without the need of mortar. They speak of times in which they shielded you, and the family you showered hospitality. Of the small plot of land around you in which lambs and cows sheltered from a winter gale. They wind and twist around the gnarled oak trees that shade you. That provided cover for a last resting place. The half-dozen or so crumbling headstones, the inscriptions on which are now indecipherable, hold their secrets fast.

You hold dear the precious remembrance of a people long since gone – and barely remembered? Whose lives were rooted firmly in the land on which you stand. A people who embraced the precarious gifts of Mother Earth, a Mother wrapped tightly among the trimmings of a concrete belief in One who died on a cross. A people who valued and treasured a simple life, one devoid of the trappings their descendants believed indispensable. A people whose very existence depended on neighbour and friend.

Today you are abandoned but you do not grieve.

Dare I – a mere visitor to your land – presume to utter a salutation? Dare I presume you give a damn?

I reluctantly stood, glanced back at the house in a final farewell and continued my walk.

Reaching the end of the Gap at about 5 pm, we sat for a while, looked down at the Black Valley and headed back. The return journey only took one and quarter hours – much easier as most of it was downhill. When we returned to Kate Kearney's Cottage, we relished a pint and a meal – salmon. Of course.

We drove to Killarney and then back to Lissyclerig.

I slept well that night, dreamt of all I had seen over the last few days. Resonated with a different shade of seeing.

Eleven

During the summer months, numerous arts festivals are held throughout the whole of Ireland. The *Fleadh Cheoil Chiarrai* – *Fleadh* (festival), *Cheoil* (music) *Chiarrai* (Kerry) Kerry Music Festival – was held in Kenmare on Friday 18 June. There was an opening ceremony in the Square at 7 pm and culminated with a closing Ceili at 10 pm on the Sunday. People from all over Kerry came to Kenmare for this annual celebration.

The opening event comprised a fancy dress competition and parade throughout the town which was led by pipers. After the opening speeches, there followed an outdoor concert of *Ceillí* (dance) bands and an Irish dance exhibition by local Kenmare award winning dancers. The evening closed with a *Ceillí Mor* – big *Ceillí* in one of the hotels. I saw something I had wanted to see all my life. Down the years, I had seen Irish dancing on stage, and had purchased a video many years ago of Michael Flatley's *Lord of the Dance* and watch it often. But I had never witnessed what is called set dancing, the closest thing to square dancing. However, what makes set dancing so fabulous is the speed and, most of all, what the dancers do with their feet. They all have special shoes, something like tap shoes, and, coupled with the music, the sound of their feet work was intoxicating.

Another lesson learned: down the years, when we held parish dances and when we went to Irish concerts, I was always fascinated at the way Tom moved his feet. Whilst watching the set dancers, it all clicked – his feet moved in the same way.

On Saturday, I went to the local school, attached to the church. in which were held the music competitions – fiddle, *bodhrán*, accordion, whistle, harp, flute, and *Uilleann* pipes. The competitions, attended by literally hundreds of competitors from all over Kerry, were held over both Saturday and Sunday. For 5 Euros I was able to purchase a pass which lasted the whole weekend. The age range of the competitors was from under-12s to those 18 years and over.

Next to the *bodhrán*, a favourite traditional Irish instrument of mine is the *Uilleann* pipes. They are the characteristic national bagpipe of Ireland. Their current name, earlier known in English as 'union pipes', is a part translation of the Irish term *píobaí uilleannn* (literally, 'pipes of the elbow), which derives from their method of inflation. The bag of the pipes is inflated by means of a small set of bellows strapped around the waist and the right arm. The bellows not only relieves the player from the effort needed to blow into a bag to maintain pressure, but also allows relatively dry air to power the reeds, which reduces the adverse effect of moisture on tuning and longevity. Some pipers can converse or sing at the same time as playing. They are distinguished from many other forms of bagpipes by their tone and wide range of notes: the chanter has a range of two full octaves, including sharps and flats, together with the unique blend of chanter, drones and 'regulators'. The regulators are equipped with closed keys which can be opened by the piper's wrist action thus enabling the piper to play simple chords, giving a rhythmic and harmonic accompaniment as needed. The chanter can also be played staccato by resting the bottom of the chanter on the piper's thigh to close off the bottom hole and then open and close only the tone holes required. If one tone hole is closed before the next one is opened, a staccato effect can be created because the sound stops completely when no air can escape at all. They are almost always played sitting down.

As well as the second day of the music competitions, there were stalls down the main streets of town. One of the stalls was manned by a Traveller man who entertained the crowd with dozens of hand-made puppets. He picked them up one by one, spoke in a different tone with each one, told stories and sang. He was superb. There were also lots of buskers. Upon the large stage set up in the Square, different bands and street theatre actors performed.

From about 2 pm on the Sunday several competitions were held, two of which particularly ensnared me. The first was a beer barrel competition, one for women and another for men. The competitors had to push a beer barrel along a designated course, the winner the first over the line. This was followed by a sheaf tossing competition, again one for women and one for men. The sport of Sheaf Tossing is believed to be over 300 years old and consists of two high poles over 18 metres high with a seven metre crossbar between them. The sheaf-tosser uses a hay pike to toss a sheaf, which is usually made of rushes, over the cross bar, the highest thrower the winner. Both of these competitions lasted over five hours!

Tossing the Sheaf

It was wonderful to be surrounded by locals for a change instead of tourists. It was a festival for the local Kerry people, rather than something put on for tourists. The bars were all open and people swamped the streets, drinking and enjoying the festivity. I was impressed that, even though there was a lot of street drinking over 8-10 hours, there was no evidence of loutish or objectionable behaviour. Just a lot of talking and laughing – and drinking. Tom, who had spent the afternoon watching a game of Gaelic football at home on the TV, joined me in town about 7 pm. We had a meal and then went to the final *Ceillí* in one of the pubs, in which I rose and joined. Well, somewhat!

From June 24 to July 4 the Killarney Summerfest was held. It comprised outdoor concerts in Fitzgerald Stadium and was headlined by international stars Bryan Adams, The Coors and Kris Kristofferson as well as a wide range of international buskers including James Maguire and Melissa McCarthy from Australia, a musical duo who fused their Irish and Australian musical roots to create their own unique sound, which incorporated the didgeridoo. There was a host of street entertainment, children's workshops, art exhibitions, classical music. New to 2004's Killarney Summerfest was a banner-making project run in local schools, with the resulting banners on display by businesses throughout the town. There were regattas, guided walks and a ring of Kerry cycle event.

We attended a step-dancing workshop which was held in a room of the Dromhall Hotel from 2 pm – 4 pm; just for beginners like myself.

'But I don't need a beginner's lesson,' Tom cried.

'Come on, Tom, do it for me.'

My God, I didn't know I was so out of shape. But I recovered and that night we went to a *Ceillí Mor* in which I participated yet again. I needed more practice on the feet work. I actually thought Tom needed more as well!

In the Gleneagle Hotel, we attended a performance named *Tráthnóna Bothántaíochta*, which followed the lively and important tradition in remote *Gaeltacht* – Irish speaking areas – centred on an evening spent going from one house to another where music was played, stories told, songs sung and poetry recited. Although I could not understand a word spoken, it was most enjoyable. Tom translated as much as he could without missing out on too much of what was being said.

Also of much interest was an exhibition of traditional and environmentally friendly crafts called *Féile Enviro*. I watched some guys in the process of building a *curragh* – the famous rowing boat used by so many Irish fisherman years ago. They were very light, of variable size. The one under construction seated eight people. They have a wooden frame and hide stretched over the frame. Because of their lightness, the men could carry it ashore, very suitable around the rugged west coast and out at the islands.

Prior to my arrival in Ireland, I had hoped we might be able to attend the Bloomsday celebrations in Dublin on 16 June, which, in 2004, was the 100th anniversary of James Joyce's classic *Ulysses*. Unfortunately, that did not happen. Next time!

In Killorglin, set on the Ring of Kerry, the Puck Fair (*Aonach an Phuic*) – reputed to be Irleand's oldest fair - is held each year from 10-12 August.

Puck is the name given to a male goat. The most widely mentioned story relating to the origin of King Puck associates him with the English Ironside Leader Oliver Cromwell. It is told that while the 'Roundheads' were pillaging the countryside around Shanara and Kilgobnet at the foot of the McGillycuddy Reeks, they routed a herd of goats grazing on the upland. The animals took flight before the raiders, and the he-goat or 'Puck' broke away on his own and lost contact with the herd. While the others headed for the mountains, he went towards *Cill Orglain* (Killorglin) on the banks of the Laune. His arrival there in a state of semi exhaustion alerted the inhabitants of the approaching danger and they immediately set about protecting themselves and their stock. It is said that in recognition of the service rendered by the goat, the people decided to institute a special festival in his honour. Every year a group of people go up into the mountains and catch a wild goat. The goat is brought back to the town and the 'Queen of Puck', traditionally a young school girl from the local primary schools, crowns the goat 'King Puck'. The 'King' is then put into a small cage on a high stand in the middle of the town square which signifies that the festivities may begin.

I had recently read about Puck Fair by John B. Keane, of Listowel fame. I looked forward to yet another festival. Traditionally, it was an Irish horse and cattle fair, a time for people to sell and buy, for women to show their produce and for friends to meet and socialize.

I was initially horrified by what I saw.

Sure enough the hapless goat was there. But there were also dozens of stalls selling the greatest amount of plastic rubbish and trashy toys imaginable. The pubs were over-flowing, the streets littered with rubbish, beer bottles and cans strewn everywhere. It seemed nothing but a drink fest and an opportunity to market gaudy trinkets. Surely, I mused, the ancients of Killorglin would be turning over in their graves.

We did not stay long: after a meal in Killarney we returned to Lyssiclerig about 10 pm.

Although very tired, I found it hard to sleep. Reflecting on my disappointment, I began to wonder if maybe I needed to revise my previous musings about the fair. For sure, Puck Fair is an inheritance of old fair days. Those days are long gone. A vacuum had materialized. But isn't our own Royal Show very similar? Did not the Royal Show originally provide an opportunity for people to show their animals, display their home-made wares, to congregate and socialize? And, although there is still that element, hasn't a degree of gaudiness crept into this with its hundreds of show bags full of trinkets, its side-show alley and such like? As I admitted that perhaps I needed to lessen any judgement, I gradually fell asleep.

One could have a hard time in deciding which fair to go to each weekend during those summer months. They cater for all ages and tastes. Opera and drama, music – traditional, classic and pop – art, fishing and angling, dog hunts. You name it, the Irish have a festival for it. I heard people speak of the opera festival in Wexford City. Singers from all over Europe flock to the festival. The singing, the dancing, the drama all overflow into the pubs after the performance. Of course, it does not cost a fortune to procure the best singers from Europe. Not like in Australia, where we are forced to pay a fortune to acquire accomplished artists.

The Irish are also fortunate in as much as the country is so small and the rural areas are not so depleted of people as in Australia. It is no big deal, for instance, for someone from Co. Kerry to travel north to Co. Sligo for the weekend. At most, one would only have a four to five hour drive. The people think nothing of it.

Other occasions for celebration are the many religious feasts throughout the year. It was quite an experience being in a predominantly Catholic country, very different from secular Australian society. Every day, twice a day, death and funeral announcements are made on the radio and where and when the requiem Mass will be held. Also, on the radio at both noon and 6 pm there is the recitation of the Angelus.

Sunday 13 June was the Feast of Corpus Christi which was celebrated with Mass at 8 pm followed by a procession through the streets of Kenmare at 9 pm. I was flummoxed. A religious procession through the town streets on a Saturday night? The procession was led by a group of young girls decked out in their white frocks and veils, followed by a group of altar boys and then the priest who carried the monstrance in which was encased the Blessed Sacrament, a consecrated Host of bread which Catholics believe has been transfigured into the Body of Christ during the Mass. Four men held a golden canopy over the priest. The people followed in their hundreds. We recited the Rosary and sang all the old hymns with which I had grown up: *Sweet Sacrament Divine* and *Soul of my Saviour*.

All the shop fronts and hotels were decked out in silver and gold bunting; many shop windows were decorated with religious artifacts and plants and flowers. It took about an hour to complete the procession and return to the church where we participated in the ritual of Benediction.

Whilst joining in the singing of the hymns and relishing the carnival atmosphere, I could not help but think of days of long ago…

As a young girl in a primary school which was run by the Sisters of St. Joseph of the Sacred Heart, I mourned the fact that at every religious ceremony in which most of my female classmates were decked in their white dresses and veils, I was not allowed to join them. I was too tall, I would stand out – and that, certainly, was not appropriate! I would sit in the pew with my family and, with an ache throughout my whole body, gaze upon the saintly girls throwing their rose petals on the floor as they preceded the altar boys and the priest. For my First Communion day, my maternal grandmother, whom I adored, was determined that I would present as regal and dignified and, certainly, above the rest of the class. She bought my veil. It was huge and bloomed around my head. Sister Patricia was horrified. We had steadfastly rehearsed in the days leading up to the Big Day; we knew exactly who was to sit where, the limited space we were expected to take up in the pew. Sister Patricia did not take into account my Nana's determined resolve. My veil took up so much extra space that confusion reigned and all our rehearsing was negated. But, eventually, Sister Patricia solved this problem; she dragged me out of my designated position and led me to the back of the rows of girls and sat me down beside her. I turned my head, looked towards my family. Nana was beaming.

Poor Sister Patricia! She was not aware that this … this …girl who had upset all her plans was to do so once again before the Mass was over. As the time came for us to stand and humbly walk towards the altar rails, I started to panic. Goodness, have I confessed all my sins? Was my soul spotlessly clean in order to receive the Body of Christ? Surely not. I must have missed some undisclosed misdemeanor. Would I not be struck down by lightning as I held out my hand to receive the Sacred Host from the priest's saintly hands? Sister Patricia stood, beckoned me out into the aisle. I hesitated.

'Come on girl, you've done enough already to wreck the day. Hurry up!' Sister Patricia hissed. I demurely obeyed, was astonished that no streak of lightning burst through the church roof. At the end of Mass, when we paraded outside the church, the steadfast gleam on Nana's face demolished any remaining inward guilt.

The Feast of the Assumption – a ceremony which acknowledges that Jesus' mother, Mary, was assumed body and soul into heaven on her death – was celebrated on Sunday 15 August. I had been looking forward to the tradition a pilgrimage to Our Lady's well just outside of town after Mass, but it did not occur. It was possible that the walk around the Holy Well did not take place because the Feast coincided with the monthly Fair day in the town. After Mass at 12 noon, we walked into town, had a light lunch and went for a walk around the Well by ourselves.

As I have previously related, I did appreciate the opportunity to engage in the local community's various activities, not as a tourist, but as someone who enjoyed a closer connection.

And then, of course, there is sport.

Early after my arrival, Tom said he had some tickets to the Gaelic football match between Co. Kerry and Co. Cork, to be held in Killarney. Would I like to go? Why not! I had five brothers but knew absolutely nothing about rugby, football, cricket, soccer. I am possibly one of the few Australians who do not go wild during the AFL Grand Final. I spontaneously decided to play nine holes at my local golf course in Perth one Saturday. I couldn't understand why there was hardly anyone on the course. It was a glorious Saturday afternoon in September. Where was everyone? It was not until I finished my game and went up to the house that I learned the answer to my complex question: yes, it was Grand Final Day.

I dressed carefully – donned a red T-shirt and fawn calf-length trousers with a wide white stripe. Tickets to the game; that surely meant we would be seated in style in one of the grandstands. We drove to Killarney about midday, only to realize we should have left a lot earlier. Cars were everywhere. We had to park a long way from town and join the throng of people as we made our way to the oval. People dressed in various configurations of red and white kept coming up and slapping me on the back. An equal number of people were decked out in yellow and green.

'What's going on here?' I asked Tom. 'Why do all these people keep slapping me on the back?'

He nonchalantly looked around, then towards me. He casually remarked that it might be 'cause of the colors I was wearing'. He looked around again and then informed me that Cork colors were red and white.

'You should be wearing Kerry's colors; see, they are yellow and green.' Thanks, Tom, really appreciated that bit of information.

Comfortable seats in the grandstand? No way! We were perched on a small rise to one side of the court, standing room only. The tide of ovation continuously swamped me; the roar, the chants, the cursing and swearing – 'Fack this! Fack that!' – the cheers, the euphoria. It was not an important game, or so I thought; 'twas not a final or anything like that. Is this what all football matches are like? From the little I had seen of Australian football, Gaelic football seemed quite different: there was no tackling, no violence. Kerry won. Tom told me that Cork is the biggest county in Ireland and doesn't like losing.

After the match, 32,000 people swarmed the streets of Killarney and parties went well into the night. Traffic was closed off as the crowd drank and sang. I soon learned that this was standard practice at the end of a game, in whatever county it was held – football was not just a game, it was a time of togetherness and celebration as well. Typically Irish?

During our travels, Tom would often ensconce himself in a bar with a good pint on a Sunday afternoon to watch the weekly match. I was quite happy to leave him to it and partake in a bit of exploring on my own. I soon learned that nothing was important enough to stop a fellow from watching the game.

As with the Arts Festivals, I was greatly impressed by the number of people who would drive long distances to watch games in the various counties. Again, Ireland is so much smaller than Australia, and there are towns and cities throughout the country. Not the vast emptiness of the land beyond our cities. Although I did not go to another game, I did become slightly interested in the results of the weekly matches. Shortly before my departure, on a Saturday drive to Killarney for some last minute shopping, I walked down the streets and shouted out 'Up the Kingdom!' to the many Kerry fans who flocked the streets.

Up the Kingdom! How on earth did an Irish County football team acquire that motto?

Kingdom?

Twelve

Soon after my arrival in Ireland, Tom asked me if I wanted to go with him to pick up his car – it was being serviced, and the mechanic had lent him a car in the meantime. I thought Tom meant that we would be just driving down the road into Kenmare. No way! We drove for about an hour and a half through tiny picturesque villages into Co. Cork. The drive was lovely, but I kept thinking what a long way it was to drive to a mechanic. We finally arrived at a place called Clonbannon Cross, a true crossroad. There are only three buildings there: the garage, a tiny shop and a pub.

The mechanic's mother lives above the shop and manages it. The shop is about as big as my bathroom! As in all things Irish, we had to wait about an hour before the car was ready. I got to talking to the mother – Breda – who took me inside and made me a coffee. She had lived there for 50 years, arriving there as a bride. When she moved in, there was only the shop and the pub: her parents-in law owned the shop and her husband later built the garage. When Breda first arrived, the shop opened straight onto the kitchen of the house. Her in-laws had eleven children in this tiny house. By the time Breda moved in with her husband – who had by this time opened the garage – living in the house were her in-laws, Breda and her husband and three of his siblings. Breda had six children.

Breda now lives on her own: husband passed away and her children have moved on. She relishes her freedom and loves serving the customers. As Catholic as they come, there is a grotto to Our Lady in the garden, pictures of the Sacred Heart everywhere in the house with candles aflame underneath – even in the bathroom. At the top of the stairs of the small cottage is another altar to Our Lady. She was an amazing woman, 79 years young. Not a line on her face, dressed in a plaid skirt with a wicked grin and lilting laugh.

The pub next door has *Curtin* boldly emblazoned across the door. Breda told me, quiet nonchalantly, that it was the house in which John Curtin, Australia's war-time Prime Minister, was born. It was not until I returned to Australia when I discovered that John, the Prime Minister, was actually born in Australia. It was, indeed, his father, also John, who supposedly was born in the old house, sometime around 1854. But then, what's wrong with such a small mistake, at all at all? I would have loved to go into the pub, but Breda was too interesting, so I thought I could go another day.

During the long drive back to Kenmare, I came to a deeper understanding of the Irish soul. Of course Tom would travel all that way: they are his friends and there are many hours of daylight in the long day. At all the little tranquil villages we passed, people were sitting outside, chatting and passing the day. What better way to spend time. In Australia, I am always so rushed, I would never think of driving 90 minutes to a mechanic and then drive back home. Will I ever slow down?

A few days later, Tom had to register his car in Tralee, the capital city of Co. Kerry, which is on the way to Listowel. I was very excited as we had made arrangements to call upon John Foley's sister, Mary and her family. Tom's childhood friend John was the person of whom I was made Guardian, after his stroke when Tom retired to Ireland in 2001. Mary was very glad to see me and had a great spread waiting for us.

The fortitude of women like Mary and Breda amazed me. Mary had lived in her house, about six and a half kilometres from town, for 45 years. She also arrived in the house as a bride. I had seen some pretty small cottages and hers must have been the smallest. Her stove was right at the front door – when I walked into the house, I almost fell into the oven. Besides the front room – kitchen, dining and living room combined – there were two small rooms off it. No laundry, no bathroom. As a bride, she looked after her mother-in-law for five years and had four children. For the past 17 years she has looked after two grandchildren.

Two women who had lived in the same house for 45 and 50 years! I had moved house twenty- three times in 18 years.

Mary was one of the happiest women I'd met. She has her brother, John's, sparkling blue eyes. Her husband, sadly like so many, was an alcoholic. He worked for the Main Roads and used to bicycle into town. One night, whilst riding home, he fell off the bike, banged his head and died.

On hearing Mary's story, I had remembered what I had read in Tralee in the Council House whilst Tom was re-registering his car. I looked around and read a notice: *Request for Driving Licence*. Under a heading – *Disabilities and Diseases* – it said: *A medical report is required if you suffer from any of the following*. The first on the list? Alcoholism. Although it did make me smile, I also felt sad. Another thing I had noticed, in churches, shops, etc., were the many advertisements with venues and times for meetings of Alcoholic Anonymous. On reflection, I did not necessarily see this as a pointer to the Irish being more prone to this sad disease. We are all aware how prevalent it is in Australia. Rather, I wondered if this said more about the Irish acceptance of the need to address the problem up front, instead of pretending it does not exist.

After we left Mary, we returned to Listowel and booked into a B& B. Listowel is a renowned literary centre, the home of John B. Keane who wrote *The Field* [eventually made in film]. Keane was a prolific writer of all things Irish. He lived above a pub which he ran and wrote of life and characters that flowed through the bar. Although he has passed away, the J.B. Keane pub is still there and we went in for a whiskey and a light meal. A couple of weeks previously, there was the Listowel Writer's Week Festival. Like all the towns I had previously seen, the church is the focal point. The Catholic Church and the Church of Ireland look at each other across the square, vying with each other for prominence. However, the protestant church is now closed and has been turned into a theatre which stages many of J.B. Keane's plays.

The next day, we continued to drive north to a place called Ballybunnion which is on the mouth of the River Shannon, the longest river in Ireland. It is not on the tourist route but is a favourite place for the local people to go for a holiday. It has the most fantastic beach, or strand as the Irish call it. It is about four and a half kilometres long and a half kilometre from shore to sea. The sand is very flat. We walked the length of the beach and back – about nine kilometres in total. Whilst walking, I reflected on the difference between this and Australian beaches. The sand there is coarser and so retains water: when the tide goes out, the sand does not dry out. Therefore the wind does not ruffle the sand. A big event each year is the Ballybunnion horse races: they race on the strand.

Along the cliffs above the beach are two 18 hole golf courses. World famous, they are called link courses and world championships are played there. At the entrance to the town there is a statue of Bill Clinton, gold club in hand. In the club house, where we went for a pint, there was a big photo of Tiger Woods.

After our walk, we went to the bath house and had a seaweed bath. For only 13 Euro (about $A20) we immersed in baths – in separate cubicles – with a large bunch of seaweed in it. The oil from the seaweed was so beautiful, very curative for aches and pains. I luxuriated in it, soaked right up to my neck. After my bath, I spoke to a woman who filled me in on the history of the place. It is one of the few beaches in Ireland that is not gravel, and in the 1920s there was a separate part of the beach for women bathers and another for men. The part of the beach where the baths are is separated by a headland, which originally separated the two bathing areas. On top of the headland, there is the remains of an old castle or fort, which looks right over the Atlantic – very forbidding.

We then drove south to the Dingle Peninsular. It is heaven on earth. Dingle is a vibrant fishing port. Nearly all of the peninsular is what is called a *Gaeltacht Area,* and most of the roads and other signs are in Irish only, unlike the rest of the country where they are in Irish and English. I loved Dingle. It combines my two loves: mountains and the sea.

Following a lunch of local fish and chips, we drove west to Dunquin and caught a boat out to the Great Blasket Island, the largest of the islands west of Ireland, four and a half kilometres from land. Over 1,100 acres of unspoilt largely mountainous terrain, the Great Blasket is approximately six and a half kilometres long and one and a half kilometres wide. Besides the Great Blasket, the most westerly point in Europe, there are four other smaller islands. The Blaskets had been inhabited for over a thousand years and only in 1953 were the last few remaining inhabitants evacuated to the mainland.

In the past the whole group of islands was referred to as Feiritéar (Anglicised name – Ferriter) Islands. From the end of the thirteenth century, the Feiritéar family leased the islands from the Earls of Desmond and from Sir Richard Boyle after the dispossession of the Desmond Geraldines at the end of the sixteenth century. They retained a castle there; unfortunately there are no physical remains of the castle because the stones were carried off to build the Protestant soup-school in 1840. That school was closed down in 1851 after the ravages of the Great Famine.

The last of the Feiritéar to control the Blaskets was the poet and rebel-chieftain, Captain Piaras Feiritéar. Some critics have argued that his Irish poetry shows the influence of the English Elizabethans. He was hanged at Cnocán na gCaorach in Killarney in 1653 after he and his followers were defeated during the Confederate Ireland wars nearby at Ross Castle. The word 'Blasket' is a mystery. No one knows when or who first gave it that name. The names 'brasch', 'brasher' and 'blaset' are recorded on contemporary Italian maps of the fourteenth and fifteenth century. The name 'Blascaod/Blasket' has all the characteristics and resonances of a foreign borrowing and it has been suggested that it originated from the Norse word 'brasker' – a dangerous place.

We alighted from the boat, no mean feat as there was no pier, just the rock ledge used by the old islanders, and spent a couple of hours on the island. The island was coated on top with a covering of furze and heather, with peat or bog beneath much of it.

The Islanders survived on mainly fishing, a few ridges of potatoes, and a patch of oats or rye. Some of them had a cow or two; others who had none would depend on a drop of milk from the neighbour who had a cow. The land is poor and sandy around the houses and their plots would have been scattered here and there. A year's supply of manure would not have gone far on the smallest of holdings, and the dung had to be supplemented by material from the beach: mussel shells and seaweed. At times it is said that soot from the chimney was spread as fertilizer.

The mountain was held in common by all the islanders, with turbary rights and a right to hunt the plentiful supply of rabbits. The expression 'right of turbary' means a right to cut and carry away turf from the bog-land and includes the right of preparing and storing on the bog-land any turf cut therefrom. There was an unwritten rule in force regarding the grazing of sheep: 25 sheep for each grazing cow, and the man who did not have a cow was not allowed to graze sheep on the mountain.

The village itself was divided into two sections: the lower and upper village. There was a slight edge to the competition between them. It was believed that life was nobler in the lower village. Tomás O' Criomhthain and Muiris O' Súilleabháin lived there as did Peig Sayers when she married. In due course, Peig moved to one of the new houses in the upper village. Both Island poets, Seán O' Duinnshléibhe and Micheál O' Súilleabháin (great-grandfather of Muiris) lived in the lower village. The best musicians and singers lived in the lower village. In these noble pursuits the lower orders, so to speak, had the upper hand on their neighbours above! Even so, the upper village had its own distinctiveness. Pádraig O' Catháin, the King, lived in the upper village

The shells of the old houses still stand, a testament to the people who eked out a meagre living. They kept alive a rich oral tradition of story-telling, poetry, song and folk tales and a way of life almost vanished today. Seven people, men and women, had books published by Oxford University Press over a span of 100 years. They were, of course, all written in Irish. I spoke to a woman and she told me that in her school days, one of the books, written by Peig Sayers, was used to study Irish. The houses, about a dozen, were built quite close together, providing intimate community living. It would be a hard, bleak place in winter, lashed by the fierce Atlantic winds and ocean tides.

The Blaskets

I learned that over the last ten years or so, people have been going there for weekends. It is possible to camp on the island for a day or so and there was accommodation for about a dozen people: rudimentary, dormitory style, but clean and dry. A German woman went over each summer, from May to September, and ran a simple café where residents could get breakfast and vegetarian meals. There are no trees on the island and water has to be carried over from the mainland. It would be a good place to go for 24 hours: 24 Euros per person overnight, which included breakfast.

I could not help but think that it was a great pity that the people were evacuated from the Blasket islands. Surely they could have been encouraged by the Government to stay. Now, 50 years later, great efforts are being made to resurrect Irish traditions, in many instances perhaps too late. In the 1950s, of course, things were a lot different. Ireland had only been independent for 20 years, the Celtic Tiger had not been born, there was a lot of hardship and poverty and immigration was enormous. The young people – especially the young women – did not want the life their mothers had, did not want to go on the land, let alone marry onto the islands. Young men and women migrated in their thousands.

On reflection, I realised that they could not be blamed or judged in a way: life was hard. The Blasket community had dwindled to only about 15 people and there had not been a marriage on the island for 20 years. I still could not help think what a shame it was that, now in the beginning of the 21st century, the government and people wanted to reclaim something that was perhaps lost.

The amazing thing, of course, is that, when I was in Ireland, the tourist industry was huge and would have been a major contributor to the economy. They naturally wanted to see the 'traditional' Ireland of their fantasies. Perhaps I was part of that? In the big tourist centres, as I had observed, much was done to present a traditional face. I could not help but think, for the most part, that it was a mask. In the pubs, with the music and the cráic, the customers were predominately tourists, not the young people of Ireland.

This was a reason why I was so lucky to have Tom's place to stay. I had not been forced to rely on the tourist track and had the opportunity to see beyond the mask, beyond which the people were wonderful, friendly and helpful. I enjoyed seeing and being a participant in the efforts to revive the true Ireland and not just the Leprechaun face presented to the tourists.

On our arrival back on the mainland, we visited the Blasket Centre, a wonderful set-up that explores and shows the history of the islands. There were many such places around the country run by the Heritage Association. They are authentic museum-type places and areas of education and learning. Previously, we had each bought a Heritage Card which allowed us unlimited access, for 12 months, to all Heritage listed sites. Often there were videos as well as written and visual information.

We continued along the Peninsular and visited the Gallarus Oratory, built in the sixth century, the best preserved early Christian church. Shaped like an upturned boat, it overlooks Smerwick harbour. It represents the apogee of dry-stone corbelling, the stones laid at a slight angle, lower on the outside than the inside, which allowed water to run off easily. At the Gallarus Centre, Tom partook in a spirited discourse with the guy in attendance – all in Irish. As mentioned, Tom is quite good at speaking Irish and enjoys the opportunity to speak the language. It is a lovely sounding language, very soft. One thing I noticed: when speaking Irish, all traces of brogue are gone, only evident when English is spoken.

We also saw ancient bee-hive huts, relics of the Celts, who were very prolific in West Ireland. Again, they were made without mortar. The ancient people lived in them and some were used as places of worship.

Beehive Hut

I was disappointed in our visit to a Celtic and pre-historic museum. I had hoped it might show something of Celtic life, but it was mainly exhibits of stone and metals and other artefacts. The house in which the museum is held, however, was fantastic. The owner was from Massachusetts in the USA. He opened the museum and lived in the other half of the building.

On our drive back to Dingle, where we planned to stay the night, I suddenly called out to Tom, 'Stop the car!' There along the side of the road were about three caravans, a rope tied between two trees upon which was draped some clothing and a small group of women, men and children enjoying a meal.

On his return from a holiday in Ireland in 1998, Tom gave me a copy of a book, *The Road to God Knows Where* by Sean Maher. It was first published by The Talbot Press in Dublin in 1972; the edition Tom brought back was published in April, 1998 by Veritas Publications, also in Dublin. The sub-title of the book reads *A Memoir of a Travelling Boyhood*. I fell in love with the book: Sean's boyhood memories, tales of his parents and large extended family, his inexplicable desire for some form of education, his need to travel on his own despite his loneliness and ache for his traditional way of life. His journey to God knew where.

I wrote a letter to him, in which I shared my delight in his book together with my praise and admiration of his relentless walk on his journey. I enclosed it with a letter to Veritas Publications with a request that, if possible, they pass the letter on to Sean. One night, my telephone rang.

'Hello,' I said, with my eyes glued to the television.

'Is that Elizabeth?' a deep male voice bellowed through the phone. It was Sean; he had indeed received my letter. He could not believe that he was speaking to someone who had read his book 'all the way in Australia!' I turned off the television, poured a good drop of red. We had a long chat. Over the next few months, we exchanged letters. When Tom went back to Ireland in 1999, he visited Sean in his small unit in Dublin. Sean's letters stopped arriving. One of the things I had looked forward to in my trip in 2004 was to try and locate him. Unfortunately this did not happen. I can only presume that he had passed on.

Irish Travellers or *Pavee* are a traditional nomadic people of ethnic Irish origin who maintain a separate language and set of traditions. They live predominantly in the Republic of Ireland as well as having large numbers in the UK and the United States. From the 2006 Irish census, it was determined that 20,975 dwelt in urban areas and 1,460 in rural areas.

The historical origins of Irish Travellers as an ethnic group has been a subject of academic and popular debate. Such discussions have been difficult as Irish Travellers left no written records of their own. An analysis of DNA from 40 Travellers was undertaken in 2011 at the Royal College of Surgeons in Dublin and the University of Edinburgh. The study provided evidence that Irish Travellers are, indeed, a distinct Irish ethnic minority, who separated from the settled Irish community at least 1000 years ago, and that such distinction mirrors that of Icelanders from Norwegians. There is evidence that by the 12th century, the name Tynkler and Tynker emerged in reference to a group of nomads with a separate identity, social organization and dialect. The word Tynker most likely arose out of the people's main source of income as they travelled the countryside: repairing tin dishes, cooking implements and such. Irish Travellers speak English and one of two dialects of Shelta and Irish Traveller Cant, which derives from Irish Gaelic and is a combination of English and Shelta.

Queen Elizabeth I passed a law that forbade people from Little Egypt entrance into England. In Europe in the eleventh and twelfth centuries, it was generally assumed that the European travellers, the Romany people, had originated in the Middle East, an area then referred to as 'Little Egypt'. Various versions of the word 'gypsy' are derived from the word 'Egyptian'. The Irish Travellers are sometimes referred to, in a derogatory manner, as Ireland's gypsies.

'Why are we so different from the buffers?' Sean writes of a question he once put to his mother.

'It's hard to say, son,' she answered, 'but us poor travellers have been on the road for years and years and years, as long as I can remember, and my parents, God rest them, never wanted to be like the buffers. We were always proud to be travellers and always will be.'

A collection of papers presented by various speakers from the Parish of the Travelling People during a forum of P.A.C.T.T. –

Promoting Attitudinal Change Towards Travellers – was collected and, in 1993, was published as *Do You Know Us At All?* Delores O'Sullivan wrote:

> *Culture can't exist on its own. Culture exists only in people. Society wouldn't survive without culture. Culture dictates how society co-operates, in securing food, in who does what in society, in how to keep warm, and in how to produce offspring. So culture is the ideas that people have in common. A Society is a group of people who share a common culture and language and are sufficiently different from surrounding groups to form a distinct group.*

Another speaker, Michael McDonagh, spoke of the nomadic lifestyle of Irish Travellers. '*I live in a house and have done for a long time but that doesn't make me a settled person. A lot of settled people travel more than Travellers do and that doesn't make them travellers.*' Nomadism entails a way of looking at the world, a different way of seeing things, a different attitude to accommodation, to work, and to life in general. Travellers see accommodation as a stopping place, whether the stay turns out to be a long one or a short one. Whether living on a halting site or in a house, any kind of accommodation is seen in a temporary capacity.

As a nomadic people, family is of supreme importance and includes, of course, extended family. Michael informed his audience:

> '*Travellers do not wander aimlessly, with no precise goal to meet. Travellers' Nomadism fulfils many functions vital to our very survival. Travellers travel in small groups, a couple of closely related nuclear families, but we understand our family membership in terms of the vast extended family. When we travel, we meet up with other family members, often with a social occasion such as a wedding or funeral, involving a family member*

as the focus of the get-together. Even families who are sedentary for most of the year feel a lot of joy and happiness when setting out on a journey, although it may only be a short one. These feelings are very much in evidence in the way Travellers are participating in the annual Traveller Pilgrimage.'

The extended family is a co-lateral relationship, one in which every adult member is informed of and consulted about major decisions. No person, young or old, is encouraged to leave the group, probably because they would not survive on their own in the wider, settled community. Children are trained to regard the family as the most important structure in their lives and to see themselves not as individuals but as part of a family. Most marriages are arranged by the family. If a girl marries a non-Traveller, she is to some extent leaving the group. Her children will have a dual identity.'

On a quiet evening, after a day of profitable 'mooching', Sean enquired of his friend's mother why she had not picked her own husband.

'Well, indeed, son, 'tis not as easy as that. Matchmaking is a very old custom with the travellers in Ireland. The reason for matchmaking is to ensure that a pavvy beor (travelling woman) marries a pavvy fean (travelling man) and not a buffer (settled person). Now when a sublia (lad) and laceen (girl) on the tober (road) come to courting age, they are thought of as being in danger. You see a girl or boy might fall in love with the first one they meet. If it wasn't for the buffers there would be no problem; but the one great fear of the pavvies is that their children might fall in love with heartless buffers and, make no mistake, to the travellers all outsiders are heartless people. It is known that when a pavvy married a buffer they are made to lead a comeragh's (dog's) life.'

Travellers spend their time being Travellers, which means consolidating family bonds by visiting, consulting, swapping, dealing and reconnoitring. In modern times, as the work of traditional Tynkers has become unnecessary, they became involved in work that can be completed in a short time: laying tarmac, lopping trees, potato picking, as well as recycling waste discarded by the 'settled' community. Whilst many Traveller parents would like to see their children learn skills which would give them opportunities for employment in factories and settled businesses, they also recognise that involvement in such activities would eventually affect Nomadism and thus the survival of Traveller culture.

There has always been a large degree of disparity and resultant antagonism between Travellers and 'settled' Irish, as is seen in all human societies, such as class differences and white people vs. darker skinned people. It is still evident today. The Commission on Itinerancy pushed the concept of rehabilitation in the late 60s and early 70s. However, when proposals for a new halting site or group housing scheme was mentioned, a group of 'settled' residents would often protest against the idea of Travellers living in their neighbourhood. Travellers do not see themselves as 'itinerates'; whilst they call themselves Travellers, they also see themselves as indigenous Irish.

Their Faith is extremely important to them, a mixture of ancient Celtic Christianity and Irish fable and myth. Sister Cathleen McDonagh directed a group in exploring the faith expression of Travelling People. 'It is hard to find the right words to use. Our Faith is part of what we are. It is as much a part of us as our very life-force. God is a very real presence in our life. If you see life as a journey or a road, then for us God walks the full journey beside us. God is with us every step of the way.' Indeed, one may remark, wasn't Jesus himself a Traveller, and isn't he the Son of God, truth?

'Hundreds of years ago in Ireland,' so said Hannora, the principal story-teller, one night as Sean huddled closer to the fire, 'when there were no such things as cars and engines, the travellers led a particularly lonely life. One night, when a travelling woman and her young children and relatives were mourning the death of her husband who died suddenly, a blind stranger came into their midst. He was dressed in a long, flowing white robe, and had equally long white hair, which had a silvery sheen that reflected the light of the goat-grease candles. Most remarkable of all was the serene look on the old man's face and, in particular, his piercing blue eyes. Perched on the old man's right shoulder was a piebald bird, a magpie.

'He addressed us: "My brethren of the road, I am deeply moved by your great sorrow and I would like, if I could at all, to try and lessen the heavy grief of your heart."

'Of course, no one could guess how such a person could relieve the widow's sorrow.

'He continued: "I see not your faces, for eyes to see I do not have. Instead my heart feels every ache and pain of such loss as yours, humble broken-hearted mother. For my sight I have here, on my shoulder, the bird of sorrow.

> *Of such birds I have seven:*
> *One for sorrow,*
> *Two for joy,*
> *Three for a girl,*
> *Four for a boy,*
> *Five for crosses,*
> *Six for losses,*
> *And seven for a secret never told."*

'Then God bless the mark,' continued Hannora, 'as if from out of thin air, another bird perched on the shoulder of the old man and, as if by magic, not one felt sad but instead everyone became happy.

' "Ah," said the old man, "the second bird has come, so you will not feel unhappy or sad now; soon three more birds shall come, then your late husband will lie in his final happy rest with a cross to mark the spot." '

Hannora continued to tell how within a very short time three other magpies appeared and how, without question, all the people at the wake made the grave and buried the dead man. Having done so, they put a little wooden cross over the grave. There was no more sorrow. After a very happy and enjoyable meal, the old man began talking again, without any prompting from his astonished, but eager and happy listeners.

"In a while now, two more birds shall come, making the total seven, and seven is for a secret never to be told. I know only too well that you are curious to find out who I am. To find out this, though, you are bound, by the appearance of the seven birds, to reveal the secret to none other than the people of the road.

"I have been on the road for many, many years, indeed for many, many centuries. Now I am feebled by my great age and blindness; but though I shall soon roam the roads no more, my birds, the magpies, shall continue in my place and all the travellers meeting them shall know whether sorrow or joy shall come their way. These birds will be a sign for travellers so that they can remember me and will also warn them in advance of any sorrow or joy.

"Now," the old man said, "as you can see, the seven birds are here, so it is time, and you shall be the only family that shall ever know my true identity. Many who follow will try to discover who I was, but only you shall know. One day, however, centuries hence, others will get to know the secret, and then, and only then, will there be happiness in the heart of everyone in Ireland." '

After a pause, Hannora said, 'Well, that's the end of the story, and to this very day no one knows who the old man was. The travellers who met and spoke to him so long ago brought the secret with them to their graves.'

'Who do you think he was?' asked Sean.

'I don't know,' replied Hannora, 'but some people have said it was St. Patrick, others said St. Kevin, and some have even said it was the travellers' patron, St. Christopher. One thing, however, everyone is sure of, is that the man was a saint.'

Who are these dark, mysterious people
So recently come to our shore?
They say they're the Lords of little Egypt
But they look so ragged and poor.
We'll harry them off as fast as we can,
And give no peace to the Travelling Man.

With letters from popes and dukes and earls,
These strangers clutter our land,
But, citizens, give them not bread nor meat
Though they say they'll read from your hand,
But pass some laws to forbid this land –
We'll give no peace to a Travelling Man.

When times were hard in those lean war years
We needed men to answer the call.
And the gypsies would fight or work in the fields
For the first time equal to all –
'So use these people while we can,
But give no peace to the Travelling Man.'

Old Gyppo's alright with his carts and his tents
Though he's not like one of your own.
He's a good bloke to have with you back in the trench
But we don't need him now that we're home.
So send him off as quick as you can,
We'll give no peace to the Travelling Man.

Our new town's alright with its shiny new homes
Of new red bricks and chrome,
But some Travelling people pulled up last week
And they lived in a mobile home –
But we soon shifted them with the council van.
We'll give no peace to a Travelling Man.

This world of ours is a brand new place,
Where 'almost all' get their rights.
We can build rocket ships that'll fly through space
(But we can't build half enough sites).
It's been that way since time began –
There's still no peace for the Travelling Man.

The Travelling Man
by Nathan Lee, a Travelling Man

I would have loved to get out of the car, walk up to the families on the side of the road, say 'Hello', and ask for a photo. I didn't.

After another lovely local fish meal in Dingle, we retired early. Sleep evaded me for a long time as images of countless Irish Travellers, the indigenous people of the land of my ancestors, merged with those of the land of my birth, the Aboriginal and Torres Strait Islander people. Memories of Sean's book, his life on the road, the prejudice he suffered during his attempts to secure education, other Traveller children not being allowed in the front entrance of the local school, not permitted in the Hall and who had to slink along the wall in case they touched any of the 'settled' kids. The increased number of halting sites (caravan sites), which were originally constructed so that Travellers could have access to parking space, electricity and sanitary services and space to graze their horses, that are now blocked by huge boulders which have been placed by local councils due to the opposition from local 'settled' residents who resent Travellers in its community.

Ah faith, I think of all the bigotry and intolerance that so many indigenous peoples continue to suffer all over the world.

What part have I played in this continual injustice, I asked myself. Why have I not made an effort to get to know the culture and the traditions of Australia's indigenous people? What price have I paid for the dearth of consciousness of the wealth and fullness such awareness could have enhanced my life? Why had I not honoured nomadism as a legitimate way of life? To what extent have Australia's indigenous people suffered as their way of life was taken away from them and forced to live as 'settled' people? Why have I been so engrossed in believing I could find myself in a country that I may never see again?

The doubts, the questions, the amazing experience incurred on Great Blasket and the physical tiredness finally fused and I drifted into sleep. As I wafted into another land, a land of *Other*, I recalled the last two paragraphs of Sean's book:

I know not what lies on the far side of the hill but I know I must waddle forward, like a duck, unsure of my footing … I can journey with the rest of humanity on the road that leads to God knows where.

Life is like this, we all waddle through the short span of life. In reality, each and every one of us is on the road, and one day, please God, we shall all meet at the final mollying (gathering) ground; then the road shall end, and for some it will be a very happy molly. There too we will, by the grace of God, meet the Saviour who travelled and mollied in his humble earthly life. With such thoughts life has meaning, and with meaning I can journey with the rest of humanity on the road that leads to God knows where.

Thirteen

I had invited Tom's cousin, Peggy, to Kenmare for Sunday lunch. I wanted to repay her for the many lunches I had enjoyed at her home in Corrig. I cooked marinade chicken and one of my specialities, *nasi goreng,* Indonesian fried rice. My childhood years had been effected by all things Indonesian.

My paternal grandfather, Carl Gotsch, was of German and Scottish heritage and moved to Java in 1919, shortly after his marriage. My grandmother, Olive Churchward, was born in New Zealand. My mother, Margarita, and her two sisters, Leonore and Karina, were all born in Jogyakarta and the family lived there for about 17 years. Papa was a cellist and was conductor of the Sultan's orchestra and also formed his own jazz band. Walter Spies, the famous Russian/German artist, was a close friend of my grandparents. Walter, who was born in 1885, came to Java in 1923, when my mother was three years old. He lived in Jogyakarta and then moved to Ubud, Bali in 1927. In those years, Java was a mecca for many artists and musicians from Europe and Walter is often credited with attracting the attention of Western cultural figures to Balinese culture and art in the 1930s and he influenced the direction of Balinese art and drama, by bringing in a more global aspect. My grandparents and their artistic friends went to Bali twice a year for holidays. My mother had told me many stories of the men walking through the mountains naked whilst my grandmother and the other women held their parasols in lady-like manner at all times.

My grand-parents and their three daughters moved to Sydney in 1936 after my grandfather suffered a stroke and was unable to play his cello for about two years. They were among the lucky few who left Java prior to the invasion of the Japanese: many of their friends ended up in Japanese concentration camps. As a German national, Spies was arrested and deported. However, a Japanese bomb hit the ship that was carrying him to Ceylon, and because the crew was reluctant to evacuate the Germans without a corresponding order, most of the prisoners on the ship, including Spies, drowned.

And so, I grew up with a love of Indonesian food.

Peggy only picked at the rice: thank goodness I had also boiled some potatoes, just in case. After lunch, with Tom and Peggy installed in front of the TV to watch a football match, I went for a drive.

I headed off to Kilgarvan, about 10 kilometres east of Kenmare. I wanted to visit a traditional Irish craft shop I had seen in passing on another occasion. *Not open today* a sign on the door read. I didn't want to go back to Lissyclerig, so branched off a side road and drove south.

What pleasure and surprise awaited me. The road eventually wound over a range of mountains which I was later to learn were the Shehy Mountains and then descended into the most glorious, green, silent Slaney Valley. Whilst driving, I was aware of something strange happening to me. I stopped the car, got out, looked around me and the tears flowed. What was going on? There was magic around me – me, the lonely, winding mountain road and the valley. It all became too much. My tears – were they for joy? Peace? Contentment and connection?

It surprised me, the deep sense of correlation I experienced. Whilst I had always wanted to visit Ireland, I was not prepared for the depth of bonding I underwent so often in my travels. I had at all times cognitively respected the Australian Aboriginal belief in, love of and oneness with the land, but had never really understood it, had never undergone a similar spiritual experience.

Slaney Valley

As I looked down upon the valley, and walked through an abandoned old farm house with its aged, stone walls, it was like some unseen force was pulling me, as if it was the burial place of family. Of course, that is what it was. That land – that country – was my spiritual home. I felt so intensely at peace and in harmony with the land. Yes, my soul definitely was formed there, eons ago.

That part of the country was all deserted long ago. Privation, famine, emigration had all wreaked vengeance. Only the mountains stood in silent testimony and held together the sons and daughters of the people of old.

It was mid-afternoon on a late winter's day in 2006. I was participating in a writing retreat on Rottnest Island, 20 kilometres west of Fremantle in Western Australia. Separated from the mainland when ocean levels rose, it was known by local Aborigines as *Wadjemup – land across the sea*. In the late 1830s, a prison for

Aboriginal men was established on the island and some 3,400 were imprisoned there until its closure in 1903. There are two old burial grounds on the island: one in which the Aboriginal prisoners were buried, which is now recognised as *sacred ground*, and a small cemetery set aside for those of European descent. There are only 13 names known of the few buried. The predominant number of children's names gives witness to the harsh conditions on the island in the early years.

I sat in the serene solitude, looked down upon the cemetery, took up my pen ...

They came, back then, in 1853,
foreheads frowned, heavy tread -
scuffed, scraped my crinkled skin
dug deep into my womb.
Sprinkled Holy Water,
chanted their strange tongue.
Buried him, Luke Ankerman.

They stood awhile. Pronounced me hallowed ground.

Could not they hear the music deep within
that which they were trampling?
My heart, deeply embedded in their grasp, pulsated
a sacredness, mine by right,
bestowed on me by timeless divinity.

For eons past I've lived and breathed,
writhed, groaned, given birth.
I AM! The Holy One, Mother Earth.

Sun blessed, rain bathed, wind caressed.
In love and harmony, formed this land,
wove a timeless tapestry.

My swollen girth raised up high
mountains, hills, glens and dales.
My breasts oozed water of life,
baptised, consecrated living spirit.

They came again. Thirteen times they came again
to this wee patch they disdainfully claimed
the only place of hallowed ground.
Disregarded my eternal gift: resurrection.

The last time they came,
they gave me you, Patrick William O'Donaghue.

Shackled minds inhibit their capacity
to understand the ongoing mystery beneath their feet,
prevent them from knowing
it was my dust from which you came,
my tender hand that pushed you forth.
For such a little time, ten short weeks.
Welcome home.

All eventually return to me.
I purge, cleanse and then release
unfettered spirit, breath and hope.
In my heaving bosom, a haven, you shall lie
a little while. Wait patiently, you'll soon be free.
You are not alone. Rest assured, I AM, I AM!

Have always been hallowed ground.

I Am, Reflections on Rottnest Cemetery

After writing the first draft of my poem, I went and sat on the beach. Together with my love of mountains, I can sit on a beach for hours, not needing any company, conversation or other distraction. I am quite content to just gaze with awe upon the ocean: ever constant, ever changing. One of the many things I loved about Co. Kerry in Ireland was the proximity of the mountains and the sea, my two great loves.

As I sat and twisted my hands through the warm sand, I reflected on the words I had jotted down. I realised that, for me, the land has always been hallowed ground. As a child, I had my own special tree in the back yard, an old English Oak. My brothers knew it was mine and dared not climb it without my permission. I loved to climb it especially on windy days and, after reaching the top of the tree, would hang on tightly to the closest branch and allow my body to be swept back and forth by the wind. I was also allotted a small patch of garden by my father: I could grow what I wanted. I thought I would grow some vegetables and then sell them to my mother. I did not make a lot of money but I did enjoy the attempt.

I relish the time spent in the garden in the later years of my life. The overwhelming sense of 'groundedness' I experience as I plunge my hand into the earth, turn the soil over, prepare a hole for a new planting as well as in the simple task of weeding. This feeling of being 'absorbed' by the soil is especially healing after a stressful time or a long day at work. Or other times when a deep longing for 'absorption' overcomes me.

Yes, it has always been hallowed ground.

I looked forward to our planned journey east through Co. Cork and then up north along the east coast of Ireland.

We travelled east to Kilgarvan and turned south through 'my valley' and on to Gougane Barra, the old oratory of St. Finbar, the patron saint of Co. Cork. Born in Templemartin, near Bandon, sometime in 550, Finbar was originally named Lóchán (modern form, Loam), he was the son of an artisan and a lady of the Irish royal court. He studied in Kilkenny, where the monks named him Fionnbharr – white head – because of his light hair. He is also known as Bairre and Barr. On completion of his education, he returned home and lived for some time on an island in the small lake then called Loch Irce, now known as Gougane Barra, the source of the River Lee, its mouth in Cork City.

Legend tells of a visit to Rome where the current pope wished to consecrate him a bishop. Finbar notified the pope of a vision he had in which that honour had been reserved by God and that he had already been consecrated in heaven. He settled for about the last 17 years of his life in the area then known as *an Corcach Mór*, now Cork City, where he gathered around him monks and students. This became an important centre of learning, giving rise to the phrase *Ionad Bairre Sgoil na Mumhan* – Where Finbarr taught let Munster learn – which is the chosen motto for today's University College Cork. He died at Cell na Cluaine in September 623 at the age of 73 years while returning from a visit to Gougane Barra and was buried in the cemetery attached to his church in Cork City.

A circular stone wall, which surrounded a grassed compound, stood beside the ancient ruins of the oratory at Gougane Barra. The walls were about three metres thick. Cut in to the wall, from the inside, were ten hermitage cells in which the monks lived. They were just high enough to stand in – dry but they would have been very cold.

On our return to the car, we saw that I had locked the keys in the car. There we were, in the absolute middle of nowhere! What to do? Evidently my prayers were heard and a young couple drove in to the valley to see the hermitages. Fortunately, the guy was able to open the car. Whew!

On our way to Cork City, we detoured to visit the village of

Blarney, famous for its Blarney Tweed – and, of course, Blarney Castle.

Blarney Castle

The castle is set in over a million square metres of outstandingly beautiful parkland. It is a Norman style castle, built by Dermot, the King of Munster, of the MacCarthy Clan. Like all Norman castles, it was originally a fortress. A ruin now, vanquished by Cromwellian forces. What's new, I reckoned on learning this? It was Cromwell, evidently, who introduced the canon into warfare. The outside walls still stand and winding, steep, narrow stone steps lead to the top. There is the famous Blarney Stone. To 'kiss the Blarney Stone' is a long-standing tradition, intended to confer a magical eloquence.

It has been suggested that the Blarney Stone was Jacob's Pillow, brought to Ireland by the prophet Jeremiah. Here it became the Lia Fail or 'Fatal Stone', used as an oracular throne of Irish kings – a kind of Harry Potter-like 'sorting hat' for kings. It has also been said to be the deathbed pillow of St. Columba on the island of Iona. Legend says it was then removed to mainland Scotland, where it served as the prophetic power of royal succession, the Stone of Destiny. When the King of Munster sent five thousand men to support Robert Bruce in his defeat of the English at Bannockburn in 1314, a portion of the historic Stone was given by the Scots in gratitude and returned to Ireland. Others say it may be a stone brought back to Ireland from the Crusades – the 'Stone of Ezel' – behind which David hid on Jonathan's advice when he fled from his enemy, Saul. It is also claimed it was the stone that gushed water when struck by Moses. It has been believed that it was a witch, saved from drowning, who revealed its power to the MacCarthys.

Whatever its origin, whatever the magical eloquence I might receive, there was no way I was going to climb all that way and not do what was expected: kiss the Blarney Stone. With the assistance of a charming fellow, I lay on my back, leaned my head over the rampart and, wow! I kissed the stone. Finally, I had secured an explanation for the blarney I have been constantly accused of!

Surrounding the castle are some lovely walks. One such walk leads to Rock Close, a meander through what was once a Druidic place of worship. They have stood the test of time, for over two thousand years: the Druid Altar, Witches' Kitchen, Wishing Steps. I took quite a few photos of gnarled, ancient trees – sycamore and oak – literally growing out of rock.

The walk helped me to recover from the nightmarish experience of leaning backwards so high in the air, and we retired to the village for a pint and sandwich and then headed for Cork City. What on earth, I pondered, was I to do when I returned to Australia, without having my daily pint? I could not see myself popping into a pub in Australia – it wouldn't be the same. Oh, woe is me!

Cork City was founded by St. Finbar. The River Lee flows in the middle of the city and divides it in more ways than one. The Northside is very steep, the roads rising straight up from the river, at more than a 45 degree angle. The Northside is the disadvantaged area whilst the Southside is more affluent. The shopping centre and Cork University are on the Southside.

As we walked through the lower Northside, close to the river, the scene was very dreary and reeked of poverty and want. The houses were grey, hard to differentiate from the thick grey clouds above, tightly packed in narrow, winding streets. My imagination ran rampant. In days of old, I figured, the smell from the river together with the fog would have seeped up the narrow streets, and multiplied the damp and despair. I visualised ragged, barefoot children tossing a stone along the road. The book, *Angela's Ashes*, came to mind, although that story was set in Limerick.

The Southside presented a completely different picture. While, like the Northside, the houses were made of stone, many of them were painted bright colours and were not so tightly clustered and were surrounded by shrubbery.

We spent the night in a lovely Southside suburb, Glanmire, which is about five kilometres from Cork City, with Tom's second cousin, Maude, and her husband, Jim – a lovely couple, both teachers. They have two daughters, and, at the time of our visit, the oldest daughter was employed in Boulder, Colorado, USA as a computer software designer for surgeons who practise keyhole surgery. I learned during my travels that many of the young Irish worked in similar fields. We had a great night – great food, imported wine, stimulating conversation. During the evening, Jim confirmed for me what I had surmised: the divisions between the Northside and the Southside. We topped off the night with a large Irish coffee: coffee, whisky and cream. I sure slept well.

The next day we continued east and stopped at Youghal (pronounced 'Yawl'). The town, a fishing port, is a walled town, granted to Sir Walter Raleigh by Elizabeth I. In Cromwellian times, it became a closed borough, a Protestant garrison town. I fell in love with it immediately. I was keen to explore the town, so dropped Tom off at a pub and went walkabout. Like all Irish towns, the streets were very narrow and much of the original stone walls were still standing. The picturesque, four-storey Clock Tower was originally the city gate, but was recast as a prison. Steep steps beside the tower led up to a well-preserved section of the medieval town with a fine view across the Blackwater estuary. Through the tower, in the sombre North Main Street, is the Red House. This authentic Dutch mansion was built in 1710. On my way back to pick up Tom, I glanced up and saw a sign 'J.D's Pub'. I immediately took a photo, with the knowledge that my brother, John Damien – whom we all called J.D. – would love a copy.

From Youghal we drove to Dungarvan in Co. Waterford. Dungarvan is famous in the world-wide golfing fraternity. We spent the night in Dungarvan and the next day drove to Waterford City. I was very keen to see Waterford City because of my long friendship with the Christian Brothers with whom I worked very closely in the Parish of Girrawheen. The oldest city in Ireland, it was founded by the Vikings and where Edmund Rice founded the Christian Brothers amongst the poor. It is also the place from which comes Waterford Crystal.

Unfortunately, the weather was terrible so we decided not to linger and moved on. And Tom was not particularly well. I was very aware of the constant pain, in varying degrees, Tom was suffering from his bout of shingles before my arrival in Ireland. The worst thing for shingle sufferers is stress: it increases the degree of pain. Tom did not particularly like cities – detested them, he said. He was truly a country boy at heart. What do they say? *You can take the lad out of the country, but you can't take the country out of the lad.* To walk around in a crowded city, in the rain, was not very conducive to relaxation. And I really wanted my stay in Ireland to be as relaxing and joyful to him as myself. So I was more than happy to forego some things. After all, everything that I saw, all that I experienced, was new, wonderful and awesome.

We continued north to New Ross in Co. Wexford. New Ross is on the banks of the River Barrow, which flows into Waterford Harbour. On the way to New Ross, we stopped off at Duncannon, on the Co. Waterford side of Waterford Harbour. Originally a

Viking fort, the English took it over, upgraded it and made it ready to fight the expected arrival of the Spanish Amada, which, of course, never eventuated.

New Ross is where President John F. Kennedy's family originated and, in 1968, a John F. Kennedy Arboretum was built. We didn't worry about visiting it. We did visit the Dunbrody, a replica ship that transported famine victims to the New World. My God, I had read much about the 'coffin' ships as they were called because of the large number of people who died on route. Nothing I had read could have prepared me for seeing it first-hand. The steerage passengers were below deck with up to seven people lying on a tiny wooden plank that looked as if it would be hard to place two people on. They were only allowed out on deck for 30 minutes a day. In bad weather, the hatches were closed for anything up to a week or ten days. Unimaginable horror. Of course, convicts to Australia and African slaves suffered similar fates.

We continued to drive east through Co. Wexford and visited Rosslare Harbour, about 10 kilometres south of Wexford City. Rosslare is one of the three ports in the Republic of Ireland from which ferries leave to and from Wales, the other ports at Cork City and Dun Laoghiere (pronounced Leery), south of Dublin. Passengers, trucks, buses and cars and other cargo also depart and arrive daily. I had no idea how huge these types of ferries could be. We watched one unload. After counting about 100 cars, I then lost count. Then out flowed the buses and semi-trailers – again, I lost count. I was flabbergasted.

The rain kept falling, softly but steadily, and after a well-earned pint, we headed north to Wexford City. We arrived there about 7.30 pm, hungry. We decided to find and book into a B&B before our meal. An hour and a half later, we finally found one, out in the countryside, north of the city. All the inner city B&Bs were booked, a Saturday night, cars and people everywhere. What was going on, at all, at all? The woman at the B&B we finally found told us there was a big match on that day in the city between Wexford and Offaly. Wexford won as they had done the previous weekend. Some wild celebrations, indeed. Around 9.30 pm, we drove back into the city for something to eat. In Ireland, whilst most pubs serve food, the majority of kitchens close down at 9 pm for the more serious part of the evening.

We traipsed through the town looking for a restaurant, anything that served food. Each place we approached was full with revellers. We finally found a Chinese restaurant.

As mentioned previously, it is impossible – or such was my experience – not to be caught up in the fever which surrounded sport in Ireland. In particular, football and hurling; one is as big as the other. What I came to appreciate is the great unifying force and social life it engendered – and not just for the sport-minded.

The next day we visited the Irish National Heritage Park, an open air museum that tracks the path of Irish evolution from pre-historic peoples to iron-age farmers, to Celts, Christian and Normans and their inevitable influence on Irish history and its people. From this visit and other similar experiences, I came to appreciate the vast array of influences on the Irish soul and its people; the two to four thousand years of various conquerors and the mark they made. What influence do we have in Australia other than that of the White Anglo-English culture? We have ignored the First Australians, and as a consequence, could it be said that our sense of who we are is predominately that of an extremely limited mindfulness? Hopefully, in future years, we will be open to the influences that the diverse peoples who have in the past sought – and in the present continue to seek – refuge and cognisance of their legitimate cultures. My husband was of Greek origin and I have always appreciated learning about Greek cooking, among the many other Greek influences that have affected and enriched my life.

We travelled north to Enniscorthy, a very historical town. What town in Ireland isn't, for goodness' sake. It was the seat of the largest camp and headquarters of the Wexford United Irish rebels, known also as the Wexford Pikemen; their only weapons were the pikes which they used to toss hay. The rebels had been spurred on by the French and American revolutions. On 21 June 1798, over 15,000 British soldiers launched an attack on Vinegar Hill, just outside Enniscorthy. The Battle of Vinegar Hill, as it came to be known, was the last attempt by the rebels to hold and defend ground against the British military. The battle was actually fought in two locations: on Vinegar Hill itself and in the streets of Enniscorthy. We visited Enniscorthy Castle which has been turned into a museum and the National 1798 Visitor Centre, a multi-media establishment. It told the whole story of the United Irish men and their drive for freedom.

In a short story I wrote in 2003 – which was placed first in the Australian/Irish Heritage Association's annual literary competition – I referred to the Irish convicts who were sent to Australia after the revolt of 1798 and how, after a clash with the authorities at Castle Hill, outside Sydney in New South Wales, Governor King re-named the place Vinegar Hill.

We also went to see St. Aidan's cathedral, designed in 1849 by Augustus Pugin who designed the London Houses of Parliament. It was one of the most beautiful cathedrals I'd seen. And believe me, I had seen quite a few! Notable features include the façade, a reredos, a screen behind the main altar carved from Caen stone, and a great north window with intricate stone tracery. The cathedral was subsequently renovated in line with reforms promulgated by the Second Vatican Council. It was restored to its near original design in 1994 when authentic colours, materials and techniques were used. The restoration took a year, during which time cathedral services were held at St Mary's Church of Ireland nearby.

By this time, Tom was exhausted. We found a pub, and a comfortable bench on which he could raise his legs with a good view of the huge television and bought a pint. I left him to watch the game between Co. Kerry and Co. Limerick and set off on foot to explore the town. Like so many towns, it had sprung up on the banks of a river, the River Slaney. I spoke to a couple of elderly men who were sitting on the side of the bridge.

'Hi there. You look comfortable,' I said. 'Having a rest?'

'Not really,' they replied. 'It's the time of day when the tide flows up from Waterford Harbour and isn't it the best time to catch some salmon and sea trout?'

'Ah, and to be sure, good luck to you.' My mouth watered at the thought of a good catch.

From the bridge I had a wonderful view of the town : the castle, the silent predominant feature and the town building which sprouted all around it. Whilst standing there, I reflected on how dreary I had found Cork City. I suppose there is something to be said about keeping buildings as they were – they seemed to exude something unique. But then again, I might have just been mesmerized by the euphoria of a gorgeous Sunday afternoon, looking down on the swift flowing river, hoping I might spy a salmon.

Eniscorthy

Whilst walking through the town, I passed a lovely high walled house and spoke to a woman watering her numerous pots of bright red and pink geraniums. With deep woe, she bemoaned that there had been no rain for a week! And this, in the middle of summer. Her house was part of what was the castle's stables and she had put great effort in doing it up without sacrificing its past. Lovely.

After the match, we continued north to Arklow, the southern town of Co. Wicklow, which is the county next to Dublin. We stayed the night.

I did not like Arklow. Being so relatively close to Dublin, it had grown almost into an outer suburb. There were many new housing estates, the houses all the same, each estate built by the same builder. Of course, it is very similar in Australia, with its sprawling suburbs reaching out like tentacles from its main cities.

After a short drive through the town, I was happy to head up into Wicklow Mountains, through the Avoca Valley. The BBC television programme, *Ballykissangel,* was shot in Avoca Valley. For years, I had dreamt of and idealized the Wicklow Mountains. During one of Perth's Arts Festivals, I had seen the play, *The Shadow of a Gunman,* by Sean O'Casey. It was the first play in O'Caseys trilogy, set in 1920 as the War of Independence raged. The other two Dublin plays are *Juno and the Paycock* and *The Plough and the Stars,* the latter of which caused a riot when first performed at the Abbey Theatre in Dublin: nationalists in the audience resented O'Casey's evident hostile portrayal of the revolutionaries of the 1916 Easter rising. The key event in *The Shadow of a Gunman* is a Black and Tan raid in the middle of the night on a tenement house: the sense of what it was like to be caught up in a war between guerrilla fighters and an occupying army is deeply evoked. I remember sitting in my seat in a theatre in Perth, and dreaming of being there, in the Wicklow Mountains.

Alas, I was to be disappointed. My dream did not materialize. I had imagined mountains similar to the majesty and romance of the Kerry Mountains. As we drove through and over the Old Military Road which was built through the lonely mountains by the British after the rebellion of 1798 in order to flush out rebels, I could appreciate how the rugged wilderness of the mountains and its inaccessibility provided a safe hideout for opponents of English rule. Whilst Tom drove, I keenly looked out the window, half expecting a rebel to jump out at us.

We stopped for a pint and a sandwich at the Coach House in Roundwood. Along the tops of the walls around the inside were written quotes from the Irish Masters. A few examples of the quotes:

*Between my finger and my thumb,
the squat pen rests, snug as a gun.
Seamus Meanry-Diggins.*

*An Irishman's heart is nothing but his imagination.
George Bernard Shaw.*

*Perhaps my best years are gone,
but I wouldn't want them back,
not with the fire in me now.
Samuel Becket.*

*We are all in the gutter,
but some of us are looking at the stars.
Oscar Wilde.*

I am Ireland. I am lonelier than the old Woman of Beare.

Padraig Pearce.

Padraig Pearce was another romantic figure of my youthful dreams.

I first learned of him when I was 17. I had just started nursing at St. Vincent's Hospital in Darlinghurst, Sydney. I was awfully lonely and then became ill. I have referred earlier to the Catholic priest, the chaplain to the hospital, with whom I became friends. We would spend many a magic night reading poetry. He introduced me to Padraig Pearce, an Irish hero, one of the leaders of the Easter Rebellion in 1916, who was executed by the Brittish. As I read the quote from one of his poems on the wall of the pub, I recalled a favourite poem which, to me, encompasses his seemingly tragic journey:

The beauty of the world hath made me sad,
This beauty that will pass;
Sometimes my heart hath shaken with great joy
To see a leaping squirrel in a tree,
Or a red lady-bird upon a stalk,
Or little rabbits in a field at evening,
Lit by a slanting sun,
Or some green hill where shadows drifted by,
Some quiet hill where mountainy man hath sown
And soon would reap; near to the gate of Heaven;
Or children with bare feet upon the sands
Of some ebbed sea, or playing on the street
Of little town in Connacht,
Things young and happy.
And then my heart hath told me:
These will pass,
Will pass and change, will die and be no more,
Things bright and green, things young and happy;
And I have gone upon my way
Sorrowful.

The Wayfarer.
Patrick Henry (Pádraig) Pearce

After we left the pub, I reflected that what often happens to me is that I dream about something and then, invariably, the dream does not become real. Do I have to learn – among so much else – that I need to put my dream aside so that I can see beauty in the reality? But I so relish my dreams! As we continued our drive, I gazed upon the reality of the Wicklow Mountains, allowed my fantasy to waft in the breeze and hoped that, one day, I would return with fresh, un-dreamy eyes.

Wicklow Mountains

We drove to Glendalough – *Gleann Dá Loch* – in the heart of the mountains. The steep, wooded slopes of Glendalough, the 'valley of two lakes', harbour one of Ireland's most atmospheric monastic sites. It was established by St. Kevin, who was born in 498, a descendent of the royal house of Leinster. He rejected his life of privilege and chose to live instead as a hermit. He chose Glendalough as the perfect place to enable him to fulfill his dream. He later founded a monastery and attracted many disciples. It became a notable site of learning devoted to the care of the sick and the copying and illumination of manuscripts.

Colourful legends about the Saint make up for the dearth of facts about him. A tale says that one day, when he was at prayer, a blackbird laid an egg in one of his outstretched hands: he remained in the same position until it hatched. That he lived to the age of 120 is another. He reportedly died around 618.

The settlement was sacked time and again by the Vikings, but, nevertheless, it flourished for over 600 years. Decline only set in after English forces partially razed the site in 1398. The ages of the many buildings are uncertain, but most date from the 8th to 12th centuries.

We entered the site through the Gatehouse, the only surviving example in Ireland of a gateway into a monastic enclosure. A short walk leads to a graveyard with the famous Round Tower in one corner. It reaches 33 metres in height. The cap of the tower was rebuilt in the 1870s with stones found inside the tower. St. Kevin's cross, one of the best of Glendalough's high crosses, dates from the 12th century and is believed to have marked the boundary of the monastic cemetery. While the main group of ruins lies east of the Lower Lake, the earliest buildings associated with St. Kevin are up by the Upper Lake. The two lakes are less than 1.5 kilometres apart. There, where the scenery is much wilder, one is better able to enjoy the tranquility of Glendalough and escape the crowds of tourists that descend upon the site. On a rocky spur and at the entrance to a cave overlooking the Upper Lake, stands St. Kevin's Cell, the ruins of a beehive-shaped structure which is thought to be the hermit's home. Evidently carved into a cliff, the small cave may have been used as a tomb in the Bronze Age, but it is more famous as the saint's favourite retreat. Another legend says that it was from here that Kevin rejected the advances of a naked woman and tossed her into the lake.

Glendalough

On leaving Glendalough, we continued along the Military Road, through Glenmacnass where a majestic waterfall spills dramatically over rocks, and then up to Sally Gap, a remote pass surrounded by a vast expanse of blanket bog dotted with pools and streams. At Glencree, we passed the ruins of a former British military barracks, just one of several found along the Military Road. From there, we travelled west, down into the Plains of Kildare. It is in Kildare that my great-grandfather was born although I have never been able to find the exact place.

We spent the night at a place called Naas, only about one and half hours drive from Dublin. We had decided to postpone a trip to Dublin. Tom caught up with an old friend, also named Tom, an ex-Christian Brother and we enjoyed a couple hours in a pub – where else?

Next morning we drove out into the southern regions of the Bog of Allen. Bogs fascinate me. Thousands of years old, bogs have a mystique and romantic aura, wild and free. I wanted to visit a place called Peatworld, an exhibition that explores the ecology and history of the bog. Damn! It was closed.

Fourteen per cent of Ireland is bog. There are strong concerted efforts to retain the bog in its pristine beauty and delicate ecosystem. Because there is no oxygen in the bog, things are perfectly preserved. It is like a refrigerator, and in times past the people put things like butter in the bog. Bog butter is continually being found and is still edible. People have been buried in the bog and their remains have been found, impeccably preserved, with henna coloured hair and skin like black leather. It is even possible to divulge what their last meal was. One was found to be buried over 2000 years ago and he had had wild-berries for breakfast! The wild heather found in the bog is good for threadworms and the willow herb was used during the First World War for dressing gangrene. The Irish have used the peat in the bogs for centuries as fuel for cooking and warmth.

Travelling south, we crossed the Grand Canal which stretches across Ireland from Limerick to Dublin. The Canal is a series of locks, used in times past to haul cargo and bog: it flows through the central bog areas. At Carrick-on-Shannon in Co. Leitrim, there is a modern marina which, in summer I was told, fills up with private launches and boats available for hire. The Canal also enjoys a thriving tourist industry. Unfortunately, we were too far away to see the boats.

We drove through Kildare and down to the Curragh, a vast grassy plain that stretches for more than 20 million square metres. Kildare is the main racing County, home to many of Ireland's studs and training yards. We visited the impressive Curragh racecourse and also the nearby Irish National Stud, founded in 1900 by an Anglo-Irishman, William Hall-Walker, of Walker whisky fame. He gave it to the British in 1915 in receipt of the title Lord. It was returned to the Irish in the 1960s.

Walker was an eccentric who sold horses on the basis of their astrological signs and installed skylights in the stables so the horses could be 'touched' by sunlight or moonbeams. During a tour of the stud, Tom took a photo of me hugging a horse's neck – none other than Vintage Crop, the winner of the 1993 Melbourne Cup! The reigning stud was Indian Ridge which earned $85,000 for covering a mare, and he covers 70 mares a season. Not a bad little money earner! Horses from the National Stud are often flown to Australia for stud purposes.

Inside the grounds is the famous Japanese Gardens, laid out in 1906-1910 by the Japanese landscape gardener, Tassa Eida, with the help of his son, Minoru, and 40 assistants. The impressive array of trees and shrubs include maple, bonsai, mulberry, magnolia, sacred bamboo and cherry. The garden takes the form of an allegorical journey through life, beginning with the Gate of Oblivion, the Tunnel of Ignorance, the Hill of Learning, the Parting of the Ways and on to the Gateway of Eternity.

By this time, it was late afternoon and we headed home to Kenmare. Kildare City is a very historic town, but we decided to visit it when we go to Dublin, as the road to Dublin goes right through the city. It took about four hours to drive to Kenmare, and we arrived to a deep fog. As we crossed the Kerry Mountains, yet again I felt as if I was arriving home.

When I retired and began to drift off to sleep, my erstwhile dreams of Wicklow Mountains flooded me. I offered up a short prayer: *Please. No more dreams!* I don't think my prayer was fervent enough. Mountains continued to poetically invade whilst memories of youthful readings engulfed me.

To thee, O father of the stately peaks,
Above me in the loftier light — to thee,
Imperial brother of those awful hills
Whose feet are set in splendid spheres of flame,
Whose heads are where the gods are, and whose sides
Of strength are belted round with all the zones
Of all the world, I dedicate these songs.
And if, within the compass of this book,
There lives and glows ONE verse in which there beats
The pulse of wind and torrent — if ONE line
Is here that like a running water sounds,
And seems an echo from the lands of leaf,
Be sure that line is thine. Here, in this home,
Away from men and books and all the schools,
I take thee for my Teacher. In thy voice
Of deathless majesty, I, kneeling, hear
God's grand authentic Gospel! Year by year,
The great sublime cantata of thy storm
Strikes through my spirit — fills it with a life
Of startling beauty! Thou my Bible art
With holy leaves of rock, and flower, and tree,
And moss, and shining runnel. From each page
That helps to make thy awful volume, I
Have learned a noble lesson. In the psalm
Of thy grave winds, and in the liturgy
Of singing waters, lo! my soul has heard
The higher worship; and from thee, indeed,
The broad foundations of a finer hope
Were gathered in; and thou hast lifted up
The blind horizon for a larger faith!
Moreover, walking in exalted wood
Of naked glory, in the green and gold
Of forest sunshine, I have paused like one

With all the life transfigured: and a flood
Of light ineffable has made me feel
As felt the grand old prophets caught away
By flames of inspiration; but the words
Sufficient for the story of my Dream
Are far too splendid for poor human lips!
But thou, to whom I turn with reverent eyes —
O stately Father, whose majestic face
Shines far above the zone of wind and cloud,
Where high dominion of the morning is —
Thou hast the Song complete of which my songs
Are pallid adumbrations! Certain sounds
Of strong authentic sorrow in this book
May have the sob of upland torrents — these,
And only these, may touch the great World's heart;
For, lo! they are the issues of that grief
Which makes a man more human, and his life
More like that frank exalted life of thine.
But in these pages there are other tones
In which thy large, superior voice is not —
Through which no beauty that resembles thine
Has ever shone. THESE are the broken words
Of blind occasions, when the World has come
Between me and my Dream. No song is here
Of mighty compass; for my singing robes
I've worn in stolen moments. All my days
Have been the days of a laborious life,
And ever on my struggling soul has burned
The fierce heat of this hurried sphere. But thou,
To whose fair majesty I dedicate
My book of rhymes — thou hast the perfect rest
Which makes the heaven of the highest gods!
To thee the noises of this violent time

Are far, faint whispers; and, from age to age,
Within the world and yet apart from it,
Thou standest! Round thy lordly capes the sea
Rolls on with a superb indifference
For ever; in thy deep, green, gracious glens
The silver fountains sing for ever. Far
Above dim ghosts of waters in the caves,
The royal robe of morning on thy head
Abides for ever! Evermore the wind
Is thy august companion; and thy peers
Are cloud, and thunder, and the face sublime
Of blue mid-heaven! On thy awful brow
Is Deity; and in that voice of thine
There is the great imperial utterance
Of God for ever; and thy feet are set
Where evermore, through all the days and years,
There rolls the grand hymn of the deathless wave.

To a Mountain
by Henry Kendall

Fourteen

Bags packed and everything ready for a trip up the west coast of Ireland, I looked forward to meeting Anne and Maris, friends from Perth, in Galway. They had been on holiday in Europe and had planned to come to Ireland while I was there.

Before retiring early in readiness for the trip, I sat for a few moments and looked out on Kenmare Bay, at the dappled sun on the mountains. A glorious view, so peaceful and restful. Sheep grazed on a far field, a couple of deer on the field immediately below the house. A glass of wine in hand, music playing softly in the background. Ah, what a great life! I had bought some audio tapes and had been taping quite a bit from Tom's great selection of CDs. I looked forward to playing them back in Australia and be again whisked away to the mountains.

Early the next morning, we travelled north through Tralee and up along the coast of Banna Strand. The Irish patriot, Roger Casement, landed there in 1916 from a German U-boat with a load of rifles for the Easter rising. He was arrested as soon as he landed and a memorial stands on the site of his capture. This was also the place where the movie, *Ryan's Daughter* was filmed.

At Tarbert, on the southern banks of the River Shannon, Ireland's longest river, we drove onto a ferry and crossed over into Co. Clare, and headed west. I had hoped to visit a heritage site in Kilrush, but found it closed for repairs. We stopped for a pint and had a game of pool. I didn't think any of the other players needed to worry about any competition from the two of us! From there we drove to Kilkee, a very large holiday town, the closest seaside town to Limerick.

As we continued to drive north along the coast, I could not help but think that if anyone wanted to punish me, all they had to do was to plonk me anywhere in the West Clare region. Lashed by strong Atlantic gales, we drove through flat, practically treeless plains. The occasional hawthorn tree we did see was bent over almost double, away from the wind. We stopped a couple of times to take a view of the coast and each time, the wind nearly knocked us over. I couldn't help but try to imagine the place in winter.

We finally reached the world famous Cliffs of Moher. They are indeed breathtaking, and rise to a height of 200 metres out of the sea and extend for eight kilometres. The sheer rock face provides, with its layers of black shale and sandstone, sheltered ledges where guillemots and other sea birds find rest. I believe that even when shrouded in mist or buffeted by Atlantic gales, they do not lose their grandeur. We decided not to go for a three-hour walk along the north from the Visitor's Centre or the 5 kilometre walk south. The area was packed with tourists and whilst I fully appreciated the magnificence of the Cliffs, I could not help but think of the even grander view to be seen along the Great Australian Bight. A shame that Australia is so far away and cannot attract similar numbers of tourists.

We continued north, having planned to spend the night at Ballyvaughan, on the banks of Galway Bay. About half way to Ballyvaughan, we travelled through a town called Lisdoonvarna. The Victorians developed the town as a spa, but its claim to fame now is the annual Matchmaking Festival held in the town during October. Ballyvaughan is a fishing village dotted with slate-roofed cottages. It is also the gateway to the Burren, which we planned to visit the next day.

The word Burren is derived from *boíreann*, which means 'rocky land' in Gaelic, an apt name for the vast limestone plateau. In the 1640s, Oliver Cromwell's surveyor described the place as 'a savage land, yielding neither water enough to drown a man, nor tree to hang him, nor soil enough to bury him.' Whilst it is true that few trees manage to grow survive, other plants thrive. As in eons past, Ireland was once connected to the Mediterranean coast, the Burren is a unique botanical environment in which Mediterranean and alpine plants rare to Ireland grow side by side, such as Bloody Cranesbill of the geranium family and the Hoary Rock Rose and Maidenhair Fern, which thrives in the damp crevices that cover the Burren.

Glaciation and wind and rain erosion formed limestone pavements with deep crevices known as 'grykes'. The porous rock is easily penetrated by rain-water, which has gouged out an extensive cave system beneath the rocky plateau. A quirk in the local climate means that, in winter, the hills are warmer than the valleys and hence, unusually the cattle are let out to graze on the high ground in winter.

The Burren

The Burren is one of the best places in Ireland for butterflies, with 28 species found in the area. The birdlife is also varied. Skylarks and cuckoos are common on the hills and in the meadows, while the coast is an ideal place for razorbills, guillemots, puffins and other sea birds. Mammals are evidently harder to spot. Badgers, foxes and stoats live there but it is more likely that a herd of shaggy-coated wild goats or an Irish hare is spotted.

Through the rolling hills of limestone and valleys of limestone pavement, the landscape is dotted with ringed forts and burial sites and hundreds of metres of dry stone fences. We stopped by the Poulnabrone Dolmen, a portal tomb which dates back to 2500 – 2000 BC.

Poulnabrone Dolmen

We continued south to the capital of Co. Clare, Ennis, which is pronounced *Inish*. I was fascinated to see thousands of crows picking away in the field as we approached the city. At that time of the year, the farmers have mowed their fields for silage and had them wrapped in large bundles covered in black plastic. Tom told me that very few farmers go to the bother of 'saving the hay' as was done in his childhood years. Farmers now opt for the easier and quicker method of collecting silage. After the silage is collected, the crows can get to the soil and look for worms which they can't do when the grass is long, almost half a metre high.

I loved Ennis, another medieval town which traces its origins to the 13th century; narrow, winding streets, brightly coloured shop fronts.

I almost got arrested! We attempted to drive through the centre of town. The narrow roads in the town have been turned into one-way streets but there is still not much room. Because the footpaths are so narrow, everyone walks on the road. Smack bang in the middle of town, the traffic was at a standstill. I got out of the car to stretch my legs and walked down town. Poor Tom was stuck in the car. Approximately 200 metres down, I saw about six Army guys in full battle dress with rifles drawn. I went up to one of them and asked what was going on.

'Oh, nothing,' he said. 'Just transferring some money from the bank.'

I stood back and took a photo, my camera always at hand. The burly army guy grabbed my arm and said, 'No photos, please!'

Luckily, I had already taken my shot. When I returned to the car, Tom laughed and told me that this is what happens all over Ireland because of a history of members of the IRA holding up banks when money is transferred. The traffic was held up for about 15 minutes and then everything went back to normal – Irish normal, that is. Evidently the same thing happens when trucks want to unload goods at shops. Because the towns have evolved over hundreds of years, there is no room at the back of stores for unloading cargo. We found a place just outside of town for a nice lunch of salmon sandwiches. What else!

From Ennis, we drove east to a place called Kilbane, still in Co. Clare. A friend's cousin lived there and I had promised I would call by. I had rung Kitty the night before and she told me that when we got to Kilbane, her house was across the way from the pub. Well – we drove through the narrowest country lanes, winding through hills and more farm land and drove right through Kilbane. I must have blinked! I enquired at a farmhouse and the woman pointed backwards and said, 'See that house with the smoke coming from the chimney – she has a welcome for you.'

We drove back, saw the pub and yes, her house was directly opposite. Her front door opened onto the street.

After a short visit, we drove across Co. Limerick and into Co. Tipperary to re-visit my cousin John Joe in Coolrus. How I loved saying that: my cousin. I invited John Joe and his wife, Mary, to visit us in Kenmare before I left Ireland. Mary was keen, but it turned out that John Joe was not. He did not like travelling far. What would he have thought of travelling in Australia?

The next day, we drove back through the winding road to Ennis and headed north to Co.Galway to join Anne and Maris. We met at a B&B in Oughterard, the gateway to the Connemara District. The Galway races were in full swing for a week, thus we had to drive about 300 kilometres from Galway City for accommodation. After we settled in, the four of us went for a lovely long walk down to Loch Corrib, the largest lake in Ireland. We enjoyed yet another lovely pint and meal in a pub – need I say it, delicious grilled salmon, baked root vegetables and greens.

The following morning, we drove back to Galway City. Galway is the centre for the Irish-speaking regions in the West and has a lively university in the city. Under the Anglo-Normans it flourished as a trading post. In 1396 it gained a Royal Charter and, for the next two centuries, was controlled by 14 merchant families, or 'tribes'. The city prospered under English influence, but in 1652 Cromwell's forces wreaked havoc. After the Battle of the Boyne in 1688, Galway fell into decline, unable to compete with east-coast trade. In recent years, however, as a developing centre for high-tech industry, the city's profile has been revised.

Because of the Galway Race Festival, there were thousands of people in the city. We finally found somewhere to park, had a light lunch, and then headed for the races. There, the fun began.

I put a two Euro each-way bet on a horse in the first race. It won. I continued to bet and backed the 2nd, 3rd, 4th and 5th winners. I was having a ball! Everyone was rubbing me for luck, they couldn't get over it — five winners in a row. I picked a horse for the 6th race, went to the betting ring and saw it was odds-on. I disregarded my ex-husband's voice in my head, urging me to steer clear of odds-on favourites and backed the winner. The same thing happened in the 7th and last race. From a time in another world, I'm quite okay with reading the form. Won a fortune, one may ask? No, damn it! Although I love the races, I am not a gambler and am a hesitant better. My largest bet was five Euros. But I didn't care: I had great fun and a wonderful day.

'Bugger,' Tom decried. 'We could have all become rich!'

After the races, we drove west along Galway Bay and stopped for a meal. Despite my meagre winnings, I did shout the four of us a meal of roast lamb, fresh vegetables and a lovely bottle or two of French wine.

Following the meal, we headed north and drove through the southern reaches of the Connemara before heading back to the B&B in Oughterard. The Connemara is famous as the place where Cromwell told the dispossessed: 'You can go to hell or Connacht!' It is a wild, wind-swept plateau with 121 lakes and acres of blanket bog. Truly mysterious, a primitive beauty — a land that whispers her secrets.

Anne and Maris had hired a car, so next morning we headed off in convoy and travelled deeper into Connemara territory. We visited a heritage site, which is called 'Dan O'Hara's Homestead'. In a wild, rocky setting, this farm recreated the tough conditions of life in Connemara before the 1840s. Dan O'Hara has been immortalized in song, including Finbar Furey. He lived there with his wife and three daughters and one son in a two-room cottage. He widened his window and put in glass. Immediately his rent was increased due to an Improvement Tax set by the landlord. From what the guide told us, this is where the term 'daylight robbery' was derived! I'm sure this was said with tongue in cheek – the guide had a very dry wit – but whatever, the term was apt. Dan was eventually evicted and forced to emigrate with his family. His wife and three daughters all died on board. Dan arrived in New York penniless with his young son, who was cared for by relatives and, unskilled, Dan had to resort to selling matches on the streets of New York. He died two years later.

We reached Clifden on the Atlantic Coast, the capital of the Connemara and then drove north along what is called the Sky road, a 17 kilometre road that hugs the cliffs on a high mountain slope. Unfortunately, there was a lot of mist and visibility was poor. On a clear day, the view would be magnificent.

We reach a small town called Leeane, on the border of Co. Galway and Co. Mayo. We stopped for a pint – of course! And then parted company with Anne and Maris. They wanted to head back to Galway City and we arranged for them to come to Kenmare the following week. Tom and I continued north, into Co. Mayo to a town on the coast called Westport. We booked into a B&B and then headed west along the Clew Bay to Croagh Patrick, Ireland's holiest mountain, which was formerly known as Reek Mountain in pre-Christian Celtic Ireland. Thousands of people flock there every year.

Croag Patrick

Named after the Irish national saint, the mountain is one of Co. Mayo's best-known landmarks. From the bottom, it seems cone-shaped, an impression evidently dispelled by climbing to its flat peak. The quartzite, scree-clad mountain has a history of pagan worship from 3000 BC. In 441 AD, Patrick is said to have spent 40 days on the mountain during which he fasted and prayed for the Irish.

On 17 March and Reek Sunday, the last Sunday in July, thousands of penitents, often in bare feet, make the pilgrimage in Patrick's honour. From the start of the trail at Campbell's Pub in Murrisk, where there is a huge statue of the saint, it is a two-hour climb to the top at 765 metres. Mass is celebrated on the peak in a modern chapel. The view over Clew Bay would be amazing. We climbed for about 30 minutes.

One thing saddens me: there are many religious sites in Ireland, most of them on old Celtic sites, yet little or no acknowledgement is made that the mountain was originally a Celtic religious site. Undoubtedly, Patrick's aim, of course, in choosing that particular mountain was to debunk the ancient religion. In the same way, the legend that tells how he rid Ireland of snakes is based on the reality that the snake was a holy symbol of pagan religions, religions that included worship of female gods as well as male gods. The debunking of the snake, by casting it in an evil light, was a concerted effort to debase the feminine aspect of pagan religions from as far east as ancient Israel and beyond.

I can understand, given the climate and mindset of the Church of old, that this was done to demystify old religions, but I would like to think that in today's age, the Church – and if not the Church, at least the Government – could recognise the old Celtic religions and the vast influence they had – and still have – on Ireland. Why do we still believe we have to discredit other faiths, other traditions whose richness has the potential to deepen and enhance our own experience?

We had a meal in Westport. It was a Bank Holiday weekend and the town was crowded. I was itching to hear some music so we called into a pub which is owned – and named after – Matt Molloy, the flautist from the Chieftains. It was packed to the hilt so we did not stay.

On Monday morning we travelled east through to Castlebar, and then turned south-east to Castlecrea where we visited Conalis house, the ancestral home of the O'Connor clan, the last high King of Ireland and Connaught. This old Gaelic family can trace its heritage back 1500 years, except for a period when it was taken over by Cromwell. The ruins of the 17th century home are visible in the grounds. It was heartening to visit an ancient home that belonged to an Irish Catholic family. Most of the homes I had seen were all built by English Protestants. It is a magnificent home with 45 rooms. As well as a well-stocked library, with hundreds of books that record Irish history, there was a gallery of family portraits spanning 500 years. In the billiard room is the harp once played by Turlough O'Carolan (1670-1738), a blind harpist and the last of the Gaelic bards. In the grounds of the house is the O'Connor inauguration stone, which dates from 90 BC. The home was currently owned by the 25th generation of O'Connors.

We continued to Stokestown in Co. Roscommon, a visit I have referred to in a previous chapter. Stokestown Park House, the greatest Palladian mansion in Co. Roscommon, was built in the 1730s for Thomas Mahon, an MP whose family was granted the land by Charles II after the Restoration. The house stayed in the family's hands until 1979, when major restoration began. Although by then the estate's original 12,000 ha had dwindled to 120 ha, the original interior of the house is intact.

Set in the stable yards, the Famine Museum uses the Stokestown archives to tell the story of tenants and landlords during the Great Famine. Landlords during the famine years were divided into two camps: some who were charitable and inaugurated Famine relief schemes and the callous whose only concern was to be rid of their starving tenants. Stokestown has a particularly merciless reputation: the Lord of the Manor at that time, Major Denis Mahon, evicted more tenants from his land than all of those evicted during the Famine years in Ireland altogether. He was eventually murdered for his cruelty. The current owners of the big House wanted somehow to redress the situation and opened the Famine Museum to tell the tenants' side of the story.

From Stokestown we travelled south to Roscommon City and visited yet another castle, Roscommon Castle, and then further south to Athlone, the capital of Co. Westmeath and booked into a B&B for the night. It could be said that Athlone, which owes its importance to its position by a natural ford on the Shannon River, is the centre of Ireland.

I loved Athlone. It is a very old fortress town, and the 13th century Athlone Castle lies in the shadow of the 19th century church of St. Peter and St. Paul. We watched boats come up the Shannon; at Athlone they have to pass through locks – something I had never seen before. There were lots of pleasure craft on the river as well.

We appreciated a lovely chicken risotto at a cafe called Pavarotti's in Athlone's West Bank and then went to a pub for some music. On my return after a visit to the Ladies' room, I passed a raucous American who was trying to connect with anybody and complained in a loud voice:

'Doesn't anybody drink in Ireland? I can't shout anybody a drink!'

I immediately replied, in a like manner, 'You can buy one for me.' There was a loud guffaw throughout the hotel.

As I entered the dining room of the B&B for breakfast the next morning, I went to sit down. The owner, who, with her husband, had run the B&B for 25 years, rushed up to me and took me by the arm.

'Oh, no, Elizabeth. You sit here. That one is for Tom.'

My God! I was back in Girrawheen! Many a time when Tom and I attended a family celebration for a Christening, Confirmation, etc. a special chair was always set aside at the head of the table for Father Tom; no way did I dare to up-seat him!

From Athlone, we drove south to the ecclesiastical seat of Clonmacnoise (the Irish *Cluain Mhic Nóis* means the meadow of the sons of Nós) in Co Offaly. It was founded in 548 by St Ciarán, the son of a master craftsman. Situated on an esker ridge overlooking a large area of bog through which the River Shannon flows, its location in earliest times was literally at the cross-roads of Ireland where the north/south artery of communication, the Shannon, crossed the major east/west routeway along the gravel ridges of the glacial eskers. This pivotal location contributed to the development of Clonmacnoise as a major centre of religion, learning, trade, craftsmanship and political influences. As the burial place of St. Ciarán, it has attracted pilgrims for nearly 1500 years.

On the border between the two provinces of Meath and Connacht, Clonmacnoise – which, with its large number of lay members, resembled a town rather than just a monastery – benefited from the patronage of powerful provincial kings, some of whom aspired to the kingship of Ireland. Until the 9th century the monastery had close associations with Connacht but from then until the 11th century, it was in alliance with the kings of Meath only to revert to Connacht again in the late 11th century and early 12th century. The monastery was plundered on many occasions by Irish enemies, Vikings and Anglo-Normans, but fell into decline from the 13th century on when it became merely the seat of an impoverished bishop. In 1552, the English garrison from Athlone reduced it to a ruin.

Clonmacnoise – the Cross Roads of Ireland

We continued to head south and went to the Shannon Bog Railway, still in Co. Offaly. We participated in a 45 minute rail tour of the Blackwater Bog which supplies turf to the nearby Offaly electric power Station. Need I say it again – the bog fascinated me. Unlike the bog in Connemara, which is called blanket bog and is only three metres deep, at Blackwater it is called raised bog and is eight metres deep. Blackwater has 20,000 acres of bog and 1 million tons of turf is harvested each year. An entire bronze-age village was evidently found in Blackwater Bog

In 50 years, the Blackwater Bog, which has taken 3000 years to form, will be gone. I did see on TV that groups such as the Irish Greens and the President of the day, Mary McAleese, were very active in ensuring that the bog and its unique ecosystem is preserved. I sincerely hope their efforts are fruitful.

After the tour, we headed off as fast as we could to Killarney to pick up Anne and Maris. We left Shannon Bridge at 3 pm and arrived in Killarney at 6.45 pm. We had a meal in Killarney and then drove back to Kenmare.

The next day, we took Anne and Maris for a drive along the Ring of Kerry. We only went half way and then drove back through the Ballaghisheen and Ballaghbeama Gaps. My God, will I ever see such a wondrous sight again. That country is, to me, the essence of Ireland: valleys and mountains, sheer 90 degree angles, ancient, foreboding, awesome, magical, mysterious.

At Ballaghbeama Gap, I got out of the car, stood with arms held high and just marvelled at the almost perpendicular slopes a few metres from me. The Spirit and my faithful travelling companion, *the presence*, hovered all around me. I cried out, 'God!' and almost dropped to the ground in adoration. A church is not needed when one can go to those mountains.

We returned to Killarney for a meal and took Anne and Maris to see the Liam O'Connor show, which we had seen back in June. Again, fantastic. And, again, I danced in the aisles.

On Thursday morning, I took Anne to town; she did some shopping and we had coffee in a fabulous place in Kenmare called JAM. Excellent fresh baked scones, lathered in jam and cream. I then drove Anne and Maris back to Killarney to catch the train to Dublin.

It was great to have them both, and kind of Tom to offer his hospitality. The following day I was very tired and just lazed around and did some washing. On Monday, we were finally to drive to

Dublin, my last trip, as I was due to leave Ireland on 25 August. As mentioned previously, prior to my arrival in Ireland, I had thought we might get to Dublin for the Bloomsday celebrations in June, but because Tom's car was being serviced, that did not happen. We had thought we might go there after our trip up the east Coast, but again decided to leave it. There was no way I could leave Ireland and not visit Dublin. One does not go to France and not see Paris, right? Not that I would know – don't know if I will ever get to France!

I knew it would be a wrench to leave Tom, but I was looking forward to arriving back in Australia to my family. Strange as it may sound, my soul had finally found a home, there in the mountains and the land.

I was sure Tom had enjoyed the three and a half months I was there. He certainly looked a lot better than when I first arrived. The last three years had been very hard for him and he had let himself run down: lost a lot of weight and then he got shingles, probably as a result of his weakened state. It was not easy for him to go back to Ireland after 45 years in Australia. But when his brother, Willie, died in 2000, Tom believed he had to go back and take care of the family home; he truly thought he had a duty to his parents. But it was very difficult for him at 74 years of age to make new friends. While a lot of people knew who he was – Father Tom from Australia – they were not what one would call friends. They knew who he was; they did not know the man.

I also fell into a dark hole in 2001 when Tom returned to Ireland and I, subsequently, retired from the Parish. Much of what I experienced was my issue around retirement and my lack of preparation for it. For most of my life I had worked, had a job to do, responsibilities to fulfil. I knew who I was – or, at least thought I did. My work, the many roles I filled down the years – oldest daughter, nurse, wife, mother, Sales manager, door-to-door salesperson, Pastoral Assistant – gave me what I hoped was an identity. The sudden and drastic change of waking in the morning with no set agenda to meet, no seeming purpose to the day, threw me into a spin. What was the point of getting out of bed, at all at all? The sudden departure of a dear and trusted friend … well, I thought it was very sad that two old friends were not able to reach out to each other for support and companionship in what was the autumn of their lives.

Fortunately, I somehow managed to survive that horrible time. Although it took a long time – and quite a heavy toll – I learned a lot about self-identification, and the great danger inherent in looking to identity for self-fulfilment. Or so I thought. Little did I know at the time that a *presence* was to take me on a much deeper journey.

Fifteen

We set off for Dublin on Monday morning, leaving early to avoid traffic between Killarney and Limerick City. It takes about two hours to drive to Co. Limerick to get onto the Dublin Road, and then about another four and half hours to Dublin. We had booked accommodation at Dun Laoghaire, which we had visited previously, about eleven kilometres south of Dublin. To avoid the traffic of outer Dublin, we cut across and drove through Wicklow Mountains. I was forced to upgrade my original impression of Wicklow Mountains. I had to admit that the first time we drove through them, I was probably laden down with romantic baggage which coloured the way I saw them. That second time round, I was free. They are beautiful, lush and green, and so close to Dublin. For me, though, they could not compete with the mountains in Kerry. Dubliners would visit Wicklow as we in Perth would visit Mundaring and its surroundings.

We visited Powerscourt on the edge of the mountains. The gardens at Powerscourt are probably the finest in Ireland, both for their meticulous geometrical design around Triton Lake and its central fountain, which is modelled on a 17th century work by Bernini in Rome, and dramatic setting at the foot of the Great Sugar Loaf Mountain, which is in east Co. Wicklow. Though only 501 metres high, the mountain's isolation from other hills, steep slopes and volcanic appearance make it appear much taller than it is. Popularly mistaken for a volcano, it is in fact an erosion-resistant metamorphosed sedimentary deposit from the deep sea. The house and grounds of Powerscourt were commissioned in the 1730s by Richard Wingfield, the First Viscount Powerscourt. New ornamental gardens were completed in 1858-1875 by the Seventh Viscount, who added gates, urns and statues collected during his travels to Europe. The house was gutted by an accidental fire in 1974, but the ground floor has been renovated and now accommodates an upmarket shopping centre with an excellent restaurant and café. Again, a great place for Dubliners to have Sunday lunch.

From there, we drove into the southern outer suburbs of Dublin, an area which is called Dublin's Riviera, much like Nedlands and Peppermint Grove in Perth. After we settled in to the B&B, we went for a stroll along Dun Laoghaire pier. There are two piers which encircle this south point of Dublin Bay. On a lovely warm evening, along with a couple hundred other people – families, couples – we walked along the south pier, which is about one and a half kilometres long.

As evening closed, we went to a pub for a drink and something to eat. We were served a wonderful 'tapas' plate of mixed meats, cheese and olives, fired prawns, marinated chicken and a pesto dip and a beetroot dip with slices of Turkish bread. Best I have ever had. I was feverish with excitement at the thought of the next two nights in Dublin.

Tuesday morning after breakfast, we walked to the train station to catch the Dart to Dublin. As I stood on the platform, I thought I was in Sydney! In the train, a sudden adrenalin rush hit me. I could hardly breathe. Not only was I to get my 'big city fix' – every now and then, I need to spend some time in a big city, one of the reasons I love to get over East every couple of years or so – here, in Ireland, I was to have my 'fix' in Dublin! To walk through Trinity College in the footsteps of Oscar Wilde, W.B. Yeats, Sean O'Casey and other Irish literary giants; to stand on the steps of the GPO and the Four Courts in the shadow of Padraig Pearse and the men of the 1916 Easter Uprising; to tread the cobblestones of Dublin Castle which was the hub of British clout in the days of old and in which Michael

Collins rode his bicycle in his efforts to spy and gather information; to walk up O'Connell Street, through St. Stephen's Green to see Temple Bar and join in an evening of music and cráic, and to sit in the Abbey theatre and watch the famous play, *The Playboy of the Western World*, which I found was on show. A life-long dream in two days!

Dublin

We arrived in Dublin about 10.45 and walked up Pearce Street to Trinity College. I was keen to participate in a guided two-hour walk led by history students. The first tour had already begun. I was not keen to rush in and join that tour, as I wanted to purchase a map of Dublin to follow where we would be going. I was informed the next tour, which was to include Trinity College and the Book of Kells and massive library, Old Parliament House, Temple Bar, City Hall and Dublin Castle, would start at 12 noon. I purchased my tour guide and we sat and had a coffee and sandwich and watched Dublin pass by.

We fronted up at about 11.45 for the next scheduled tour, only to be told that it had been postponed until 3 pm. Not to worry.

We paid for and boarded a Dublin tour bus, the usual double-decker bus with the roofless top floor, a hop-on, hop-off affair. The drivers gave a humorous talk as they drove – some of them sang and recited poetry in between their individual monologues. For seven euros, one could travel the bus for 24 hours.

We got off at Christ Church Cathedral, St. Patrick's Cathedral and at Guinness Storehouse, where we had a great tour of the famous brewery. This was of particular interest to me as my great-grandfather worked there before migrating to Australia. The brewery comprised of approximately 24 hectares and produced a million gallons of stout per day. The founder, Arthur Guinness, was given a 9000 year lease of the site. At the end of the tour, we went up to the Gravity Bar on the 7th floor to a complimentary glass of Guinness and feasted on a 360 degree view of the City.

We re-joined the bus, which drove through Phoenix Park, the biggest city park in the world, where the Irish President lives and where Handel's Messiah was first performed. It also holds the world's second oldest zoo, the most ancient being in London. From there we travelled past the Four Courts and I made a mental note to visit them on the next day. As the bus drove into O'Connell Street, it was about 2.45 pm and I was anxious to get off and head back to Trinity for the 3 pm walking tour. I stood to get off at the next stop and urged Tom to lead the way. Disaster struck! The bus suddenly lurched forward and Tom was thrown over an iron bar on the back of a seat and smashed his side. I thought he had broken a rib.

We staggered off the bus and into a café where we sat for about an hour. He was in tremendous pain but did not want to go to hospital. He said he wanted to get out of the city and catch the Dart to a place called Howth, which is a commercial fishing town that marks the northern limit of Dublin Bay. Why did Tom want to go to Howth? We slowly walked to the Dart Station, passed the River Liffey, the GPO and Abbey Lane. I was in a state of complete shock, Tom was in agony; I didn't dare to look at what we passed.

By this time, of course, it was peak hour and the train was packed. I looked around me as much as I could, wondered what on earth we were doing, stuck on a packed train to bloody Howth!? When we finally arrived, Tom was beat and ashen. I found a doctor who was about to close for the day. He kindly agreed to take a look at Tom. He said he did not think a rib was broken, but suggested Tom have an X-ray the next morning and he gave us a letter for the emergency department. Without seeing anything of Howth, we travelled back to Dun Laoghaire – an hour's run – got a bite to eat and tried to sleep.

The question as to why Tom wanted to go to Howth plagued my efforts to sleep. I decided not to ask and he did not offer any reason. I can only presume that, because of the amount of pain he was in, of which he never spoke, he just needed to get out of the city and the crowds. Perhaps he was aware that this accident had interrupted my longed-for visit to Dublin and rather than just go back to Dun Laoghaire, we should visit Howth?

Early on Wednesday morning, we went to St. Michael's Hospital in Dun Laoghaire for Tom's X-ray. As we waited his turn, I looked around me and could not believe what had happened, where we were. It was the bleakest place I had ever seen and I felt like we were in a dungeon. Tom finally had his X-ray – no break, thank God. He was still in terrible pain. About 11.30 am, we began the long drive back to Kenmare. I drove, which, to a degree, helped me to come to terms with the disaster. After a meal in Killarney, we arrived back at Lissyclerig about 10 pm, completely exhausted.

Tom continued to be in pain for a couple of days. We applied heat packs which helped. He was content to stay at Lissyclerig and recuperate.

To assuage my deep disappointment in missing out on seeing all I had hoped in Dublin, I spent a couple of days shopping. There were a few things I wanted to buy and take back to Australia. I loved shopping in Kenmare: it was such a communal experience, no impersonal shopping malls. Some of the shopkeepers had got to know me and greeted me by name and a lot of people nodded to me in the street. I also had a hair-cut. As I sat in the salon, I had to smile. Hairdressing salons are the same all over the world, I suspected: women chatted and gossiped, exchanged banter and woeful stories, glad tidings. But to listen to Irish women gossip – it was double the fun! It was nice, after my shopping was completed, to have a pint – and a chat. I knew I would miss that experience.

I also went to Killarney. As I drove back to Lissyclerig, up and over the mountains, the tears flooded my eyes yet again. It was all there, right in front of me – the ancient, mysterious, magical mountains, exuding permanence, soul. Three months previously, after my arrival, the rhododendrons were in full bloom. The heather had replaced them, up the mountain sides and along the roads, in various shades of purple and mauve.

The bruising and pain in Tom's side subsided within a few days. I asked him to take me to the Old Kenmare Cemetery where his parents and his brother, Willy, were buried. In the middle of the cemetery, there is a big plot in remembrance of the thousands of Kenmare famine victims. It was quite an experience. During my time in Girrawheen, in my role as Pastoral Assistant, I had been to cemeteries countless times. This was the first time I had been to a cemetery to visit a particular grave. It brought home to me how important it was to have a place to go to, to remember, to touch and be touched by. I asked Tom if he would be buried in the same plot: yes. It might seem morbid, but I was very happy to at least have that picture in my mind, the place where he would be buried. Please God, I prayed, I would be back many times before I had to think about the old Kenmare Cemetery. It was truly comforting.

In some mysterious way, the visit to the cemetery cemented the healing of any regret I had for missing out on seeing Dublin as I had wanted. As I sat on a small stone wall and looked out over the cemetery, I thought of all those people who were buried there.

Probably most of them had never been to Dublin. They would have spent their lives in the shade of the magnificent Kerry mountains. Their lives would not have been incomplete because they had not got to Dublin, had not seen the Book of Kells, Old Parliament House, Temple Bar, City Hall and Dublin Castle. I looked back over the last few months, recalled all the wonders I had seen. Wrapped by my *presence*, I quietly breathed *Thank you, Lord*.

As Tom was feeling a lot better, the next day we took a drive along the south side of Kenmare Bay through the Beara Penisular. We visited Derreen Gardens – about 40 hectares. The land was first given to Sir William Petty, physician to Oliver Cromwell, in 1657. His daughter married Lord Lansdowne. In 1866, his successor, the Fifth Marquess of Lansdowne, embarked on an ambitious plan of transforming the bare rock and scrub oak into a luxurious woodland garden. He realized the potential of the soft climate of Kerry, with its annual rainfall of 70 to 80 inches and the rare frosts, for growing the exotic plants that were pouring into Britain from plant hunting expeditions all over the world. There were hundreds of tree ferns from Tasmania and south-east Australia. The garden is now run by Lord Lansdowne's great-great-grandson.

Derreen Gardens

The Beara Peninsular is very remote. Dotted with sparsely populated fishing villages surrounded by black moorland, it used to be a refuge for smugglers, with the Irish getting the better deal in their exchange of pilchards for contraband French brandy. The vegetation changes practically every ten minutes or so, from lush rich grazing land to desolate wasteland. The peninsular, which is sometimes called Beare, Béirre and Béarra, was named after the Spanish-born wife of Eógan Mor, a legendary king of Munstar. The area is also the home of the mythical sovereignty Goddess Cailleach Bheirre, the Hag or Old Woman of Beare. She is represented by a stone on the peninsular at Hag's Head which looks out to sea, but comes across as deeply human in Irish and Scottish folklore and from one of the best known examples of early Irish poetry, *The Lament of the Old Woman of Beare*. The poem was written in the 9th or 10th century by an unknown author who Christianized this previously pagan goddess under the banner *Cailleach,* which can mean 'nun' but usually refers to an old woman or hag.

There is much debate concerning the poem's original meaning, most likely due to loss of subtle meaning in translation and the difficulty of extracting nuances from the original Old Irish. The poem is composed of many such nuances and explores contrasting states, the most obvious being that between youth and old age. The Old Woman's youth is associated with the richness of the land whilst her old age is connected with the bleakness of the grey sea. The poem also asserts a burgeoning Christian world in which paganism was becoming increasingly withered and impoverished. Cailleach says: '*I used to wear a smock that was ever-renewed; today it has befallen me, by reason of my mean estate.*'

More than poverty, the cloak suggests a change in her social and religious states. In Old Irish paganism, the beautiful cloak would be seen as one that was ever-renewed by the celebration of living. In contrast, Christianity does not even grant the wearing of it as an old smock, seeking to relegate all that is not Christian is not in keeping with its concept – at least, in those times – that a Christian must embrace poverty as a virtue. Could this be a reason why early Christian monks clothed themselves in long, old smocks? Did they wish to convey to the world that they were beyond earthly desires?

Padraig Pearce's poem, *I Am Ireland*, was whispered to me by the *presence* as we drove from Hag's Head ...

> *I am Ireland:*
> *I am older than the Old Woman of Beare.*
> *Great my glory:*
> *I that bore Cúchulainn the valiant.*
> *Great my shame:*
> *My own children that sold their mother.*
> *I am Ireland:*
> *I am lonelier than the Old Woman of Beare.*

Right down the middle of the peninsula run the Caha Mountains and there is magnificent walking country. Just before crossing the border between Co. Kerry and Co. Cork, we stopped at a pub and had a pint and a fresh salmon sandwich. Whilst enjoying my sandwich, I wondered how on earth I was to survive back in Australia without the plentiful amount of salmon. I'd become addicted! We then went down to the strand, a deeply pebbled beach. I took off my shoes and waded in the Atlantic Ocean for what I presumed would be my last time.

As we crossed the border into South West Cork, the scenery changed yet again, this time a continuous array of green pastures, farms right up the mountain side, divided by low stone walls. We drove out to Windy Point, the most western point of Co. Cork and then to Castletownbear – encircled by the Caha and Slieve Miskish Mountains – a fishing port on Bantry Bay in which nearly every second building is a pub. I was struck by the position of the church.

A cathedral-like structure, it was in the middle of town next to a pub! It highlighted for me the prominent part the church played in the past, and still does in the present. Quite a few times, on the side of the road, we saw a grotto carved out of the rock.

We went for a long walk along and around the docks and then enjoyed another meal. Do I dare say what I ate? Because this part of Ireland is such a popular place for walkers and bike riders, we met and chatted with quite a few people. One couple we talked to lived in Brighton, England; she is Hungarian and he is English. His name was David Thompson, one of the Telly Tubbies! He does some writing, so naturally we got talking books. We had some copies of *Winter has Passed*, the book we self-published, in the car and gave them a copy.

After the meal we drove over the Caha Mountains, a fantastic drive with the road snaking over the mountains and through Healy Pass from which there are fine views of Bantry Bay and the rugged landscape of West Cork. At the top of the pass is a carved crucifixion scene. Sheep grazed right up the mountainside. The road was built during the famine years of the mid 1840s, a prevalent industry during that time in an attempt to provide some employment – for which the men received a penny a day.

Ring of Beara, West Cork

As we drove down Healy Pass, we came across a lost lamb, which looked like it was barely two weeks old. We stopped the car, picked it up and put it back over the fence and hoped its mother was near.

And home to Lissyclerig.

I was due to leave Ireland on Wednesday 25 August. We had planned to go and enjoy some music, dancing and cráic on the Saturday prior to my leaving after the evening Mass. Just before we were to go to town for Mass, a second-cousin of Tom's, who was visiting for a week from America, called in to say hello. A lovely young man, Daniel, an architect. He stayed for a while and we solved all the problems of the Church – with the help of some amber liquid, for sure. Mass was out of the question, and so the visit to town.

On the Sunday evening we did get to town. Whilst most of the pubs in Kenmare cater to the tourist trade, there was one, the Atlantic Bar, which tailored to the locals. Behind the main bar was another room where people gathered to dance and sing. The band alternated between old time dancing and traditional Irish step dancing. I loved it there. I would get lost completely, imagining myself in a kitchen of old, with friends, dancing on cement floors in front of a roasting fire, whiling away a long winter evening.

Tired, enlivened, sad, happy: a confluence of emotions enveloped me as I prepared to retire for the night. In a few days I was to leave Ireland. As I did most nights at Lissyclerig, I wandered outside and looked up at the now not-so-strange Northern sky. The days were shortening, the night sky revealing itself earlier. As I lowered my head and turned back towards the house, a thought flung itself behind my drooping eyelids: what had been revealed to me these past few months? Had I found the ME that had seemed to evade herself for so, so long? I stopped, looked back heavenwards, sure the *presence* was speaking to me, perhaps attempting to calm my inner confusion. I resisted the temptation to answer any questions or sort out any confusion and went to bed. Perhaps they did not hold such importance anymore?

As I gently sunk into sleep, I remembered our climb up Mt. Peakeen shortly after my arrival in Ireland.

Sixteen

Tom stretched and rose from the couch after a siesta.

'Want a walk up the road?' he asked.

Without hesitation, I closed my book, laced up my walking shoes, hoisted my backpack complete with water bottle and camera and tied a jacket around my waist.

A light breeze teased the long grass. At the junction of the old dancing platform, we turned left into the final leg of the Kerry Way, the walker's equivalent to the famous Ring of Kerry. Following old droving paths and coach roads, the Kerry Way is a 215 kilometre anti-clockwise walk around the Iveragh Penisular, starting and finishing in Killarney. The section we entered weaves through Windy Gap before a descent into Killarney. When Tom was young, this was the route to Killarney.

'Want to climb a mountain?'

Unlike many of his countrymen, Tom is a man of few words. I halted, looked around in confusion. *What mountain?* We had been walking along the old Killarney Road for about twenty minutes without a tree to be seen. On both sides of the dirt road the land was flat and boggy, with clumps of tall grasses. To our left, in the distance, was what appeared to be a high, steep hill of rock.

'Why not! 'tis a beautiful evening.' Ah, to be sure, isn't it great we often don't know what lies ahead?

We scrambled over the wire fence and set off towards the pile of rocks with confident light steps. When we reached the base, my light steps soon turned into ones loaded with lead: the pile of rocks was no mere hill! It was so steep in parts that we literally had to climb on all fours. Before long, my fingers and palms stung with cuts and bruises from the rocky crags. No friendly vegetation reached out to help me heave upwards, a metre at a time, and every few minutes I had to stop, catch my breath and calm my racing heart. Burdened with a life-long terror of heights, my eyes flooded with tears of frustration and despair. Tom urged me on, assuring me the climb down the other side would be easier.

About half way, I froze, gripped by an overwhelming force. Tears flowed down my cold cheeks. As I crouched to rest, the *presence* wrapped her arms around me. I gulped, looked down. Instinctively, I knew we could not retrace our steps: there was no way I could climb down. No alternative other than to keep forging upwards presented itself. Monkey-like, I kept my eyes immediately ahead of me. I prayed furiously; cursed Tom ferociously.

Finally, the summit. I knelt on the flat surface which was covered with the odd patch of grass, and breathed a prayer of thanks. Windy Gap was true to its name. Whooh! Whooh! I finally found the strength to stand and clung to the metre-odd high concrete trig point as the wind whipped around me. Not dwelling too long on how this stone edifice was made and who had lugged concrete up the mountain slope, I turned to the panorama.

Peakeen Mountain, sometimes called Kilcurrane, is 555 metres high. Kenmare Bay lies serene to the west, the township nestling on its shores; the majestic Macgillicuddy Reeks and the Black Valley are to the north east, Killarney to the north, and the distant, mystical Caha Mountains to the south. Later, I learned that walkers are advised to approach Peakeen from its north east slopes in order to avoid the steep cliffs and crags on its opposite flank. Which side does the old Kenmare/Killarney Road border? The north west! If possible, I would happily debate my mother's well-worn cliché: ignorance is bliss.

Thank you, Lord, I sighed. I felt shielded and protected in *the presence's* arms.

We took photos of each other holding on to the trig point, happy that I would be able to prove we actually did it. We climbed the mountain; there was a bit of life left in two old crocks! It did not matter that later, in telling our story over a cold pint, we were laughingly told that the two old crocks were daft!

An old crock who climbed some rocks

The descent down the north east slope, in comparison, was, literally, a breeze. The wind behind me, it seemed as if it sometimes gently, often times forcefully, pushed me down the mountain, the terrain relatively free of rocky crags. My now constant friend, the *presence*, walked with me. My heart stopped racing, my breathing became normal and on the flat, I was able to sidestep the wet, boggy areas until finally we reached the road.

As we strode home, I pondered upon something that had puzzled me for a long time. Down the years, I never understood why, according to Tom's telling, the Irish panic if it hadn't rained for a couple of weeks. With Western Australia's long dry summers and years of drought, this attitude was alien to me. But from what I had seen so far – and, I was soon to learn, the same almost everywhere in the West of Ireland – I began to understand. The ground is 95 per cent rock! There is not enough soil to retain water. In Kerry at least, arguably the most mountainous county in Ireland, the rainwater flows down the rocky slopes only to flood the many rivers and streams and boggy flats. Paradoxically, there is not enough water in the soil on the slopes to withstand long periods without rain, yet in plentiful supply to ensure a bountiful amount of bog in the flat. Throughout the long summer of my stay, every time someone exclaimed 'Oh, woe is us! It hasn't rained for two weeks!' I smiled to myself. Maybe the Irish can be forgiven. Sometimes.

I was surprised, when we arrived home, to learn that our *walk down the road* had only taken four hours. While precariously clinging to an outcrop of rock during our ascent, I thought I was there for eternity! Tired, we ate simply. I bade Tom a good night, retired to my warm bed. Luxuriating in the softness, I closed my eyes and recalled a previous sojourn upon another mountain.

The soft whistle of the wind reverberated through the silence, beckoned me, invited me to open my arms, my soul. To accept the mountain's gift.

Whooooh! Whooooh!

I did not know the mountain was to be the setting for an epiphany. Many years were to pass before I fully understood the depth of the gift Ben Lomond bestowed, years in which she remained a faithful seducer, determined on complete incarnation.

On the last day of a two-week Easter holiday in the mid-80s to visit my daughter and her partner in Launceston in north-east

Tasmania, I readily agreed to their suggestion that we should climb Ben Lomond, although I had never climbed a mountain before. We left Launceston early-morning, took our time to drive the 50-odd kilometres through the Mills Plains to Ben Lomond National Park. The flat fertile plains gleamed in a Sabbath sun, the South Esk River sang. Inside the park, the road gave way to deeply forested hillocks. I noticed a stark line where the trees stopped and I wondered if this was how far the snow came down in winter. The mountain rose out of the landscape, a towering majestic sentinel. Her dark-grey dolerite columns, an image of the varied lengths of a gigantic pipe organ, stretched to the heavens, her peaks covered in cloud. At her base, Jacob's Ladder, the final stretch of dirt road, snaked round her, flirted with her.

The mountain quietly responded: I AM.

Heart pounding, I grasped my seat belt, ensured it was tightly locked, anxiously cast my eyes down the almost perpendicular drop. I prayed fervently we would not meet a car coming from the opposite direction. I did not think of Jacob's dream, of Angels of God coming up and going down, did not hear their chorus or Ben Lomond's melancholic accompaniment. I was unaware of the transformation awaiting me, in which Jacob's dream becomes my own reality.

We left the car in the empty car park of the ski village. The alpine cold engulfed me as, beanie low over my ears, jacket zipped high under my chin, staff in hand, I set my face to the rocky slopes. The steep path tested my endurance. I puffed and panted. My daughter, a few feet ahead, turned around, offered a hand. I thought back over a quarter of a century, to another place in which I also puffed and panted as I helped her on her first journey. I shook my head, resolved to make the climb on my own. I stumbled; small rocks loosened and I slid down the path. The mountain shivered in her preliminary stage of labour. I crouched on all fours, clambered her last slope. The pale autumn sun had reached its zenith by the time we reached Legges Tor, Ben Lomond's highest peak, a towering 1752 metres. I sat down, exhausted.

Gazed with wonder upon the rooftop of the world.

The vista before me was unlike anything I had ever seen; I recalled images of the desolate surface of the moon. It looked as if some giant hand had played a game of skittles and tossed and thrown, in wild abandonment, colossal slabs of rock. On hitting the ground, they had splintered, fallen on top of each other, around each other. Deep, time-worn, ice-worn fissures had fashioned cracks up to half a metre deep. The sun smiled wanly between clumps of thick cloud, sent dancing shadows over the rocky terrain. Patches of moss clung defiantly to their host. Where the ground dipped slightly and the rocks were more sparse, remnant clusters of alpine daisies in diverse shades of mauve, pale blue cushion plants and the variegated carnivorous sundew huddled. They whispered, nudged each other; stretched their faces to the autumnal light.

I accepted my daughter's proffered hand this time, picked up my staff and made my way across and around ancient rock. Head bowed, I trod cautiously. Slowly, my strides became longer, harder, surer as my confidence gained momentum and my determination to conquer this ancient land soared. On a high outcrop of rock, I paused, looked around, the world at my feet. Transported back to the beginning of time, I was all-powerful. I cried: I am Abraham!

In an instant, a thick cloud of mist descended and obliterated everything, drowned my pride. Lost in the nothingness, I crashed on a jagged rock. Another moment passed and the mist evaporated as quickly as it came. I repeated my cry: I am Abraham! My voice floated in the wind. Plunged once more into the abyss.

Whooooh! Whooooh!

The mountain sighed. She was mistress; I, her guest.

I listened not. I rose, rubbed my bruised shins, continued to cross the rock.

Whooooh! Whooooh!

I flung her invitation aside, shouted to the heavens: I am Abraham!

A blanket of mist enveloped me; I crashed yet again. I crawled towards a large overhanging ledge and huddled against its hard surface.

Her voice grew louder.

I screamed: *I will not be deterred!*

Unaware my scream stopped at my throat, I did not resonate with deeper murmurings, unanswered questions. The mist dissipated, the sun's face shone. I reconnoitred, emerged and planted my staff firmly on the ground.

I dropped to the ground, drew my knees to my chin, wrapped my arms tightly around them; buried my head. Yielded. Alone, I sank into the all-too-familiar grip of a despair that had haunted and stalked me relentlessly for the previous four years.

In truth, I knew not who I was.

A failed marriage, a grieving for lost dreams and hopes, an inability to find new directions had spiralled me into a chasm of depression. Feeble forays with varied counsellors, therapists, New Age practitioners, yoga enthusiasts had failed to shift the mist that permeated the depths of my soul. Six months prior to my Launceston visit, I knocked yet again on a therapist's door. During my third visit, he gently suggested a path I must take for healing, for a re-birthing of Self.

'In order to let go, to experience resurrection,' he said, 'you must move from a place of regret to non-regret. You must embrace paradox in order to reconcile the girl of your youth in all her naiveté, with the woman you have become.'

While his words seemed grand, I inwardly thought he was mad! All I wanted was an answer to the question: Who am I?

The mountain's voice persisted. Whooooh!

I sulked, resisted, crouched lower. Wondered what on earth I was doing, up on the desert of Ben Lomond. Wished to God my daughter would find me, rescue me, drive me down Jacob's Ladder. Take me home.

Whooooh! Whooooh!

I disentangled, scrambled to my feet, stepped out firmly on the rock.

Silence.

My daughter materialized from the mist, held out a hand. I trudged forward, a little more wary of the rock. We made our path in the stillness. Pride reasserted itself. I staggered, reassured my daughter; urged her to go forward. The cloud consumed all yet again.

Whooooh! Whooooh!

The mountain's voice rose in a crescendo then dropped to a whisper.

Cowed, my knees drawn up again, I traced a finger along the rock. Picked up a handful of loose gravel, allowed it to trickle through my fingers. Wondered: To what degree did the mountain acquiesce, in what way did she enter, actively participate, in her own metamorphosis?

Miscellaneous scraps of knowledge remembered from school-day geography lessons surfaced. The predominant igneous rock of Ben Lomond, subject to eons of assault by the earth's heat and constant action, slowly, at times painfully, evolved and threw up that on which I now sheltered. I marvelled at the mountain's patience, her compliance in a force over which she had – has? – no control, her total acceptance of the unavoidable reality that growth demands an assent to pain.

I picked up another handful of stone, rolled it through my palm. The mist cleared. I looked out over the mountain and appreciated her ever-present, continual process of evolution, her acceptance of the inevitability of change. What will she look like in another millennium? What will I look like in a comparative length of time? I caressed the rock and visualised the peeling away of an onion, curious about the secrets that lie within. The mountain declined my probe, her timeless wisdom in easy reach for those with eyes to see. Nevertheless, she encouraged me, thrust me forward.

My daughter's voice invaded my introspection. 'Come, Mother. We don't have much more time. An hour, at most.'

I took her hand, held fast and stepped out. Attempted to stifle the mountain's unrelenting voice. Enough! Please be to God! A cloud enclosed me yet again, my daughter disappeared in the mist. Predictably, I dropped.

The mist lifted. To my surprise, I perched now, not on rock, but on a soft corridor of mountain flowers. I saw what I thought must be a critically endangered leek orchid. Around me were more faded bunches of native alpine daisies and other plants I had noticed on my ascent. Was it really only an hour or so ago? I stretched out my hands, caressed the plants gently. I pondered on their fate as they await winter's doom, their certain death.

Death, yes … to be followed by a glorious resurrection next spring!

Mist. Sunlight. Mist. I kept walking; accepted the mountain's reality.

Mist …

Whooooh! Whooooh!

The sun lay low behind a cloud. The wind dropped. A hush descended on the mountain. I felt a slight stirring in my breast. What path must I walk in order to experience the healing balm of reconciliation? To what must I spread my arms wide?

I found a rock, sat down. The cloud hugged me, held me close. I wept. For the first time in years, my tears were warm, soothing. I surrendered, did not fight the tears.

The cloud rose, the sun smiled again.

My daughter smiled and held out a hand. 'Come, Mother; we have to go.'

The descent, though slow, was not as difficult as when I climbed it on my hands and knees.

'We'll be lucky if we can get down Jacob's Ladder before night falls,' my daughter said.

Ensconced in the back seat of the car, I fastened my seat belt, prepared for the palpitating curves, reassured, at that time of evening, we would not meet another car.

'Stop! Please! I want a final glimpse,' I cried.

My daughter's partner reluctantly brought the car to a halt and I stepped out. The mountain was bathed in a quiet, half-light. Heavy clouds hid her peak. Trickles of mist wove in and out of her towering columns.

In the shadow of the mountain, darkness falls quickly on Jacob's Ladder. I returned to the car, sneaked a last look. From her vantage of infinite time, the mountain re-asserted: I AM.

It was late when we arrived home in Launceston. Weary, I declined an invitation to join in a nightcap. Sleep quickly overcame me, enabled me to dream.

I floated in the land of dreams at the other side of the world that evening I came down from Mt. Peakeen.

> *Jacob left Beersheba, set out for Harem. When he reached a certain place, the sun had set. He took a stone, made it his pillow. In a vision, he saw a ladder reaching into heaven. And there were Angels of God going up and coming down.*

Countless Angels of god, going up and coming down, flooded my dreams.

I hovered over my bed, taken up in the mist. It was light, welcoming. I gazed upon countless mountains from a lofty height.

I awoke and rose from my soft warm bed and went downstairs

and out into the night. I again looked up into the northern sky. I walked to the top of the driveway and cast my eye towards Mt. Peakeen in the distance, then turned around towards the Caha Mountains we had travelled that day. Mountains stand strong; like oceans, they are ever changing, ever constant. Strains of music waft from their peaks.

I prayed words of thanks yet again to Mt Peakeen and Ben Lomond; to all the mountains we had traversed in the last few months – and, indeed, to mountains all over the world – for the precious gift they bestow.

Long ago, I emerged from the mist of Ben Lomond and in the fullness of time achieved a deep-rooted cognisance that life, of its very nature, demands a willingness to let go, to enter into death in order to experience re-birth. I embraced a realisation of the concrete possibility that I can move from a place of regret to non-regret, and the subsequent, surprising outcome: the freedom to move from one to another without any danger of being trapped in either, and thus denying that I have the freedom to move.

As I retraced my steps towards the house, I smiled. She who walks with me, my *presence* was so palpable, tenderly chose to remind me that what I had gleaned during my pilgrimage over these last few months and the wisdom I had so magnificently equally gleaned upon Ben Lomand – yet had temporarily forgotten – is not static: that Wisdom of its very nature continuously evolves.

I yawned, stretched my arms to the stars. Yet again, uttered a prayer of thanks.

Ending

We left Lissyclerig about 6.15 pm on the Tuesday. I was to board a ferry from Cork the following morning to Wales. We had arranged to spend the night in Cork at Jim and Maude's home. It was an awful wrench – I would no longer wake up to those mountains, to that view. As we drove through Kilgarvan and on toward the Cork Road, I thought I was in a nightmare. I wanted to jump out of the car.

It's an amazing sight: the beautiful Kerry mountains stop almost on the border between Cork and Kerry. I bade a final farewell to the mountains that had helped me to regain my soul.

We arrived at Jim and Maude's about 8.15 but, much to my distress, they were not there. Their daughter, Jemma, greeted us – a lovely girl, who I had not met before. Jim and Maude, she said, had to go to Belfast to see a sick aunt. I didn't want to be there, didn't know how I was going to survive the night. I went into a complete state of panic, wished we had stayed the night at Lissyclerig. It was the last night of the Rose of Tralee Contest. I did not want to spend my last night in Ireland in front of the TV and watch a beauty quest and listen to people gush over clothes and such. I went down to the village and bought a bottle of wine. Jemma prepared a lovely salad for our meal and, ashamed to admit, my panic abated somewhat after a couple of glasses of red. Thank god, Jim and Maude came home about 9.15 – I did not know they were due back. I went to bed about 11.30 and slept fitfully.

Tom and I left for Ringaskiddy, from where the ferry was to leave, about 8.30 next morning. The floodgates opened and I just could not stop crying. Tom was wonderful, held my hand and tried to comfort me. *Goodbyes*, he said, *are part of life*. Goodness, I knew that. Lord knows, I'd said enough goodbyes in my life: some were necessary, some were useful.

I don't know how I managed to walk on to the ferry: my legs were like water and I felt I was breaking up into hundreds of little pieces and wondered how I would put them together again.

After I stowed my luggage in the special hold, I walked on the top deck. I was there for about ten minutes and then saw Tom walk out of the terminal and I waved furiously, prayed he would look up. He did. I watched the main ropes as they were released; as they were wound back to the ship, they tore me to shreds. The ferry slowly pulled away from the dock. I stood there. Tom's figure became smaller and smaller. The ship turned around and I raced to the other side of the deck and Tom was still there – could he see me?

I knew it was hard for him, too. He also had had a lifetime of saying goodbye. I knew he had enjoyed the past three months, got a kick out of showing me around Ireland, something he had looked forward to for a long time. We were surely blessed. But given the fact that he had been programmed, so many years ago, to play down his emotions, I knew he found it very difficult to express what he truly felt. At least I could cry.

The ferry rounded a bend. I could not see him anymore.

I went below deck to get something to eat; I had not eaten breakfast. I returned to the deck and watched as we sailed down Cork harbour. I tuned into the countless number of men and women who stood, just like me, as a ship sailed down the harbour, men and women forced to emigrate, never to see Ireland again. I tuned into Tom as a young man, just ordained, nearly fifty years previously, sailing from nearby Cove, headed for Australia and the great unknown. I tuned into my great grandparents – how wonderful it was that I had been able to return to their homeland for them.

The sisters emerged from the sea, adopted human form.

Although quite content to live in the sea where they found shelter in the caves formed by great underwater kelp mounds, they enjoyed an occasional trip to the surface to bask in the sun. They would skip and run, search among the rocks and on the sand for crabs and pipis.

One day, as they were frolicking on the beach, a lonely hunter saw them. His name was Koolulla. He had never seen two such beautiful girls. He decided to capture them and keep them as his wives.

At first, the sisters were afraid of the man. But Koolulla kept a happy face. He did not tell them what he wanted to do. They soon lost their fear. They played all day on the beach, Koolulla and the sisters.

When the sun began her descent into the sea, the sisters said goodbye to Koolulla. 'Wait,' he said. 'I want to take you with me. You will be my wives.'

The sisters laughed. 'No,' they said together. 'We are daughters of the sea. We do not belong to any man. We do not belong to any land. We belong to the sea. And the sea is everywhere.' Again they laughed. 'We are daughters of the sea.'

Koolulla tried to stop the sisters, but they were too quick. They dived into the waves, took their sea form. Just before they disappeared, they yelled to Koolulla. 'Don't be sad. Come back one day and we shall return. And we shall dance and sing and play again.'

Wirango People
South Australia
The Sisters, Jean A. Ellis

Goodbye Tom, I voiced to the mountains of West Cork. Words cannot say properly what I feel. All I can say is thank you, thank you, thank you. For being who you are and for giving me a lovely, comfortable, warm place to call 'home' – for the great welcome – for showing me around – for giving me the freedom to be who I am. I take with me a realised love of this ancient land of my forebears, a concretised connection.

As Ireland faded into the distance, I cast one last look backwards. The sun emerged from a cloud, bathed me, pierced me with light. I raised my hand high, gave thanks to a primeval deity for a fresh consciousness that my roots are steeped in two shores. That I am who I am.

For enabling me to embrace a different shade of seeing.

The Final Farewell

About the Author

Elizabeth Brennan was born in Sydney and moved to Perth in 1973. She was the Pastoral Associate at Girrawheen Catholic Parish from 1983 to 2001, during which time she was also engaged in Relationship Education. She was Senior Supervisor with the Education section of Relationships Australia for six years.

She co-authored an auto-biography of Fr. Tom Gaine – *Winter has Passed* – in 2002. After retiring from full-time work, she has had more time to write, a passion she has held since her high school years. She has had numerous articles, poems and short stories published in various magazines and journals, many of which have been awarded prizes.

www.ingramcontent.com/pod-product-compliance
Lightning Source LLC
Chambersburg PA
CBHW071231080526
44587CB00013BA/1564